ITALY
THE W🌐RLD
VEGETARIAN

Christine Smallwood

ITALY
THE WORLD
VEGETARIAN

BLOOMSBURY ABSOLUTE

LONDON · OXFORD · NEW YORK · NEW DELHI · SYDNEY

To my Father who introduced
me to Italy, and Dan, who took
me back there.

INTRODUCTION

Italians enthuse about vegetables and appreciate them daily. At busy fresh produce markets, the respect for locally grown veg is plain to see. Customers admire newly arrived artichokes and chat at length about the exquisite radicchio before returning home with overflowing baskets.

It was at the large and buzzing market in Martina Franca, in central Puglia, where I first noticed something revealing about the price signs. They did not say 'fennel' or 'aubergine' alongside the cost (as it's obvious what the vegetable is), but the signs did specify 'Fasano' or 'Sant'Agostino' to show where the veg were grown. Some indicated 'Sicilia' or other regions, but most places were nearby and the vegetables were at their seasonal best.

Excitement over short-seasoned veg, such as asparagus, is an inspiring way to approach cooking whether you are a full-time vegetarian or endeavouring to eat less meat and fish. As with all ingredients in Italy, vegetables are important and receive serious attention because they are not the backing chorus but often the stars of the show. They indisputably shine in the recipes in this book. As a restaurant owner once said to me, 'Why are our mothers great cooks? Because they know how to shop well; they know how to recognise good, fresh produce, because that's the basis of everything.'

And having shopped well, even if you are in the fortunate position of being able to buy fresh veg daily, you need to know how to store it well; don't automatically put everything in the fridge. For example, keep your tomatoes in the fruit bowl and your garlic at room temperature. If you can, buy in small quantities, and use quickly, even if for preserving.

The preservation of vegetables in vinegar or oil is popular in Italy and olive oil especially is an important ingredient in the country's gastronomy. Many of the recipes in this book include it, not only to facilitate cooking or as a final enrichment, but as a major component. Treat yourself to a top-quality oil knowing that it will be a fundamental characteristic of your Italian dishes.

At the time of writing, vegetarian cheese is a challenge in Italy. I have lost count of the number of conversations I've had, even with chefs who offer extensive vegetarian options, about Parmesan, for example, not being suitable. But there is a slowly increasing number of cheese makers in Italy who are using non-animal rennet, so stay tuned.

A reliable, standby dish for many vegetarians is chopped, sautéed veg served with pasta. Italian culinary purists may roll their eyes at some such improvisations. No matter. This book contains different approaches for suitable pasta dishes as well as small dishes that tend to come from the antipasto course at the start of the meal. Although in many parts of the country this course may often be one dish, in some places the antipasti are almost a meal in themselves. (My record is being served 24 antipasti plates at a trattoria in Puglia, and that was before the two dishes of pasta arrived.) When you eat out in Italy, antipasti often provide some interesting choices for the vegetarian. Combining a few of these small dishes to make a substantial meal works well when cooking at home.

Typical and much-loved dishes are a big part of Italy's culture, but not every Italian is inflexibly tradition-bound in their home cooking. Some of the recipes that follow are contemporary, and some are classic dishes although they may well be variations on versions that you know. Using wonton wrappers for ravioli is far from traditional, but if they work for some Italians, then who are we to question? There are dishes here from the length of the country as well as all the seasons: from the rib-sticking, hearty dish of pizzoccheri found in northern Lombardy's Valtellina, via a pie of mixed greens from Emilia-Romagna, to Palermo's caponata on the island of Sicily.

Yet I have omitted one obvious and internationally popular dish that lends itself easily to a vegetarian version: pizza. Please don't think that I've forgotten about it (I'm a big fan of pizza), but this book is taking the Italian view: go to a pizzeria, where the *pizzaiolo* will have the right equipment and skills, for a relaxed evening out with friends, rather than making one in your own kitchen. (I've enjoyed many a pizza in Italy, but never at someone's home.)

Unsurprisingly, it has been when spending time and eating in people's homes that I've learnt a lot about how they cook. How simple and straightforward most people's kitchen equipment is: knives, chopping boards, bowls, pans, a handheld blender, perhaps machines for making passata and rolling pasta. A *puntarelle* cutter is about as gadgety as it gets.

It's been said that we often forget the relationships involved in our food, those connections between the producer, picker, distributor and seller. Eating is also, if we're lucky, a part of the relationship we have with people, and in turn the exchange of recipes often happens because of the associations we have built and nurtured. Many of the recipes that follow are based on those cooked by Italians who, over many years, have become very good friends. Others are from people I've just crossed paths, or spoons, with, for the briefest of moments. They've all been generous with their time, and advice, and they have all been enthusiastic about eating vegetables. But then this has been the case for many centuries, as stated by Jane Grigson in her foreword to the translation of Giacomo Castelvetro's *The Fruit, Herbs & Vegetables of Italy* in which she mentions 'An Italian's message to England in 1614: "Eat more fruit and vegetables".'

And while preparing them, there is another aspect to Italian home cooking that is often lost when following a recipe and respecting tradition. Namely the level of engagement needed when cooking. Don't just leave your pan on the heat, relying on a timer and trusting that when it rings, all will be as you wish. Use extra water if your hob is fierce or less oil if your pan is small. Test and taste regularly. Add more garlic, adjust the amount of chilli or reduce the quantity of herbs if you so wish. In other words, make these dishes your own and above all, have fun with these recipes.

It has been said on many occasions that Italy is not a country but a way of life. I hope this book will help you to enjoy vegetarian food the Italian way.

SMALL PLATES

FOCACCIA BARESE
BARI-STYLE FOCACCIA

When we think of focaccia, it is usually the Genovese recipe with its olive-oil-filled dimples. This is the Bari version, from Puglia at the other end of Italy, and it includes mashed potato. My friend Anna Cavaliere makes the best one I know, using a mixture of type 'O' and type '2' flours (I use flours that are more readily available outside Italy). She also uses Termitte di Bitetto olives with the stones left in – along with a warning to prevent eaters needing a 'surprise visit to the dentist'. Her husband, Vittorio, stresses the difference that excellent extra-virgin olive oil makes, and he is right.

SERVES 6-8

150g floury potatoes, peeled and cut into pieces
350ml warm water, plus an extra 50ml if needed
12g dried yeast
1 teaspoon caster sugar
400g strong white bread flour
2 teaspoons salt
150g *semola rimacinata* (finely milled semolina)
3 generous tablespoons extra-virgin olive oil, plus extra for greasing and drizzling
about 20 green or black olives in brine
about 20 cherry tomatoes
dried oregano
sea salt flakes and freshly ground black pepper

Boil the potatoes in a pan of salted water until soft and falling easily from a knife. Remove from the heat, mash until smooth, and keep warm.

Pour 250ml of the warm water into a jug, add the yeast and sugar and stir to dissolve.

Put the flour, salt, mashed potato and finely milled semolina into the bowl of a stand mixer fitted with the dough hook. Add the dissolved yeast and sugar while mixing on medium speed. When combined, add the remaining 100ml of warm water and the oil and continue mixing for about 15 minutes, until the dough is combined and very sticky. Add some of the extra warm water if needed. Cover the bowl and leave the dough to rise in a warm place for at least 1 hour, until doubled in size.

Grease a round non-stick cake tin, about 26cm in diameter and 5cm deep, with olive oil. Place the dough in the tin and leave in a warm place to prove for 30–60 minutes, until the dough springs back when touched with your finger.

Heat the oven to 200°C/180°C fan/gas mark 6.

Place the olives on top of the dough. Make small slits in the cherry tomatoes, crush them lightly between your fingers to remove the juice, and then gently press the tomatoes into the dough between the olives. Sprinkle over the dried oregano, sea salt flakes and pepper to taste. Finally, drizzle over some olive oil.

Bake the focaccia for 25–30 minutes, until golden brown, or for longer if you want a crunchy crust. Remove from the oven and drizzle some more olive oil over the top. Leave to cool slightly, remove from the tin and cut into slices to serve.

CROSTINI DI LATTUGA E FAGIOLI BIANCHI
LETTUCE AND WHITE BEAN CROSTINI

The Tuscans are sometimes known as *mangiafagioli*, meaning 'bean eaters', and white beans (*i fagioli bianchi*), usually cannellini, are popular in both Tuscany and Umbria. This is a subtle and delicate dish in which the lettuce plays a major part, so choose a flavourful variety. A good butterhead works well, as do stronger-flavoured Alpine leaves such as *cicoria bianca di Milano* (which grows to excess in my garden). Crostini made using unsalted Tuscan or Umbrian bread would be usual, but a real sourdough will also do the job. And use a good-quality extra-virgin olive oil for the final flourish. Peppery ones are widespread, but I prefer a fresh, grassy flavour in this case.

SERVES 4

Heat the oil in a pan on a low heat. Add the onion and cook gently for about 10 minutes, until softened and transparent, but not browned. Add the wine and increase the heat to high for 5 minutes, so that it evaporates but adds flavour.

Meanwhile, wash the lettuce and cut it into 2cm-wide ribbons. Add these to the pan, reduce the heat to low, and stir to combine with the onions. Put a lid on the pan and leave for about 1 minute so that the lettuce wilts. Add the beans and a couple of tablespoons of water, then heat through for 10 minutes. Season with salt to taste.

To serve, place a slice of toast on each serving plate and spoon some of the bean and lettuce mixture on top. Use a slotted spoon if the mixture has a lot of liquid, to prevent the toast from becoming soggy. Season with a grinding of black pepper and judiciously drizzle over the freshest and best olive oil you have.

2 tablespoons extra-virgin olive oil, plus extra to serve
1 onion, quartered and thinly sliced
100ml dry white wine
1 lettuce, such as butterhead
230g cooked cannellini beans, or 1 x 400g can, drained
4 slices of Tuscan bread or a good sourdough, toasted, to serve
salt and freshly ground black pepper

FLAN DI FORMAGGIO CON SALSA ALLE PERE
CHEESE FLAN WITH PEAR SAUCE

Pears and cheese are a well-liked combination in Italy, whether paired at the end of a meal or together in dishes such as this one which chef Marco Sposino cooks. If you're not a fan of sweetness with cheese, then make this without the pear sauce. The flans are rather fragile when removed from the oven, so don't demould when they are still hot.

A single flan makes a light meal or starter. Or, as a main meal, serve two flans each with a salad (and not the sauce), perhaps the green bean salad on page 49 if you're not a fan of sweetness with cheese.

MAKES 8

3 pears (any available), cored
    and roughly chopped
1 tablespoon extra-virgin olive
    oil, plus extra for greasing
500ml single cream
3 eggs
3 egg yolks
300g vegetarian pecorino
    cheese, finely grated
sea salt flakes and freshly
    ground black pepper

You will need 8 individual foil
    pudding dishes or moulds,
    about 8cm in diameter and
    5cm deep, to make the flans.

Place the pears, olive oil and a pinch of sea salt flakes in a saucepan over a low heat, and cook for about 30 minutes, until very soft. The sugar in the pears may cause them to catch on the bottom of the pan so add a splash of water as soon as you notice this, and periodically agitate the pan. Remove from the heat and leave the pears to cool a little before blitzing to a sauce with a handheld blender. Set aside.

Heat the oven to 180°C/160°C fan/gas mark 4.

In a large bowl, whisk together the cream, eggs and egg yolks. Mix in the grated cheese and season with freshly ground black pepper. Thoroughly grease the 8 moulds with a little olive oil. Spoon the mixture equally into the moulds until each is half full. Put the moulds into a baking tray and surround them with hot water from a kettle so that the water comes half way up the mounds. Bake for about 30 minutes, or until they are golden brown on top and provide some resistance when touched.

Remove the moulds from the baking tray and leave the flans to cool on a rack for about 5 minutes, or until they are cool enough to handle. They are fragile when hot but delicious eaten warm, so don't leave them to cool too much.

To serve, invert each mould onto your hand and tap to release the flan. Carefully place each one on a plate with the golden side uppermost. Put the pear sauce in a dish so that diners can help themselves. Serve straight away.

GLI SCIATT CON IL CICORINO
SCIATT WITH CICORIA

Sciatt (literally meaning 'toad'), from the Valtellina, in northern Lombardy, are extremely moreish buckwheat fritters that enclose melting cheese. I first ate these at a trattoria in Bianzone, owned by Anna Bertola. She uses a 50/50 mixture of coarse and fine-ground buckwheat flour, but I've never had any problems using just fine ground. One way to serve these is on a bed of green, slightly bitter cicoria leaves, which contrast well with the richness of the deep-fried cheese, or I often use escarole or watercress.

SERVES 6

Put the flours, salt, beer and grappa into a bowl and mix to make a smooth batter. Add water to loosen slightly if needed, but make sure that the mixture is thick. Cover the bowl and refrigerate for at least a couple of hours.

Mix the bicarbonate of soda into the chilled batter.

Pour about a 10cm depth of oil into a high-sided pan. Heat the oil to 190°C on a cooking thermometer.

One at a time, use long tongs to take hold of each cube of cheese, dip it in the batter to coat thoroughly and drop it into the hot oil. Repeat, cooking the fritters in batches and taking care not to overcrowd the pan. Carefully turn the fritters over in the oil using a large perforated spoon so that they brown all over – it will take about 3–4 minutes per batch. Set aside each batch to drain on kitchen paper while you cook the next.

Dress the leaves to taste with the extra-virgin olive oil and the vinegar. Arrange the sciatt on top and serve.

165g buckwheat flour
100g type '00' white flour
a large pinch of salt
220ml light beer
130ml Nebbiolo della Valtellina or other grappa
a pinch of bicarbonate of soda
olive oil, for deep-frying
250g vegetarian cheese, similar to taleggio or fontina, cut into 2cm cubes
a large bunch of cicoria, shredded, or escarole or watercress leaves, to serve
extra-virgin olive oil and red wine vinegar, to serve

THE REGIONAL FOOD OF ITALY

It is now widely recognised that there are significant differences between the food of the 20 Italian regions. But does the same regional variety exist in vegetarian dishes? Is there an appreciable diversity between vegetable recipes in Liguria and Sardinia, or Lombardy and Sicily? There most certainly is.

From the Alpine climate in the north, down to the ubiquitous Arab, Moorish and Greek influences in the south, the variety in vegetarian recipes is as marked as in other Italian food. It remains the case that should you travel any distance across regional boundaries, you will see gastronomic changes in dishes of all descriptions. Gradual changes perhaps, but see them you will.

That these differences persist and are embraced is helped by the fact that so many Italians grow vegetables, whether on smallholdings or by tending a modest patch at home in limited spare time. Homegrown is rarely enough to feed a family throughout the year, but it is enough to keep those families in touch with which crops are thriving and which are not: a superb year for courgettes but a tough year for spinach, and so on. It is difficult to sideline vegetables and fail to give them their due attention when you understand the trials and tribulations of their cultivation.

It's understandable that in a country where keeping time to the seasonal rhythm of fresh produce is the norm, provenance is important and locally grown veg are usually the purchasing default. For example, the Pugliese are proud of their *lampascioni*, bulbs (which taste like mouth-puckeringly bitter onions if they are not prepared properly), and the Venetians like to use a variety of borlotti bean called lamon for their *pasta e fagioli*. This does not mean that a recipe cooked with substitutions won't be delicious and enjoyable, but it won't be the same as when eaten in situ.

So, should we stop trying to recreate dishes that don't use the original and traditional ingredients? Far from it. Chef Franco Taruschio caused quite a stir in the 1960s when he arrived in Wales from Le Marche, and cooked Italian dishes using the best produce that was local to his new home. But that's a very Italian attitude: no matter the region, use local, and hence use seasonal. Your local asparagus when in season will not taste the same as wild Sardinian asparagus, but that doesn't mean that it won't be good.

People often talk about how the north loves its rice and risotto, and the south its pasta. But local pasta dishes are found throughout the country, from the *agnolotti* of Piedmont, to the *lagane* of Basilicata, and from *pici* of Tuscany to the *fileja* of Calabria. And as well as risotto from the north, Sicily's fried rice balls, arancini, are known and appreciated worldwide.

Even the north/south butter/olive oil divide is not clear cut. Many people are surprised that olive oil is not only a jewel of the south, but also of the northern region of Lombardy where the areas around the Italian lakes benefit from a micro-climate that permits olive groves, as well as citrus fruits, to thrive, and allows an unexpected quantity of olive oil to be produced.

Certain places are actually known for their vegetarian dishes and, regrettably, there is not room for all of them in this book. Tuscany gives us *pappa al pomodoro* (bread and tomato soup); Lombardy, *tortelli di zucca* (pumpkin-filled pasta); Liguria, *torta pasqualina* (an egg, spinach and ricotta pie, made at Easter); Campania, *caprese* salad (if you can find vegetarian mozzarella); Puglia *'ncapriata* or *fave e cicoria* (a purée of dried broad beans served with greens); and Lazio, *vignarola* (a springtime stew of broad beans, peas and artichokes). Of course, some vegetarian recipes are prepared throughout the country: vegetables preserved in oil (*sott'olio*) or in vinegar (*sott'aceto*), for example.

Italian pride in food can sometimes seem parochial (the word *campanilismo* exists for a reason) or admirable; after all our taste preferences and loyalties are ingrained at an early age. There's no doubt that food is critically important to Italians and their regional and local specialities engender particularly strong feelings. Happily, I can't see that changing any time soon.

CAPONATA DI PALERMO
PALERMO CAPONATA

Enzo Olivieri, a chef from Palermo who works in London, insists that 'caponata is not a mixture of any old vegetables. It's not a dumping ground of a dish for anything you have to hand'. He is certainly not the only Sicilian to feel this way and explains that aubergines or the alternative with artichokes are the only possible versions of caponata. Not that he's against a bit of adaptation: he uses honey instead of the more usual sugar and both tomato purée and passata, whereas many choose one or the other. He acknowledges that in Catania cooks add peppers, but as a true Palermitano, he asks, 'What do they know?' Be warned, and tweak this only behind closed doors.

You'll need to start preparing this dish at least six hours before you intend to cook it.

SERVES 4 AS A STARTER

1 aubergine, sliced lengthways and cut into about 3cm chunks
extra-virgin olive oil
1 onion, halved and sliced
3 celery sticks, cut into 1.5cm slices
2 tablespoons large salted capers, soaked in water to remove the salt
200g green olives, pitted and halved
1 tablespoon runny honey
3 tablespoons white wine vinegar
3 tablespoons passata (see page 159)
1 tablespoon tomato purée
1 ladleful hot vegetable stock (about 100ml)
salt and freshly ground black pepper

Place the aubergine in a colander and sprinkle abundantly with salt. Leave it at room temperature for 6 hours, or ideally overnight, to drain away the liquid and bitterness.

Take a large saucepan and generously cover the bottom with olive oil (the amount you need will depend on the size of your pan). Place over a high heat. When the oil is sizzling, reduce the heat to medium–low and add the onion. Fry for 4–5 minutes, stirring occasionally, until golden. Add the celery, then the capers and olives and stir to mix. Add the honey and vinegar, mix again, and cook for a further 5 minutes to let the vinegar evaporate slightly.

Add the passata, tomato purée and stock and cook over a medium heat for 20 minutes, until the mixture has thickened slightly and the celery has softened. Season with pepper to taste (it won't need salt because the stock, capers and olives are salty).

Remove the salt and liquid from the aubergine cubes by wiping with kitchen paper and pat dry, then fry them. Deep frying is best as they will be cooked evenly but shallow frying in a pan using olive oil is fine: take a wide, deep frying pan and generously cover the base with olive oil. Heat the oil to 190°C. Using a slotted spoon, carefully add some of the aubergine cubes to the oil, ensuring that you don't overcrowd the pan and significantly reduce the heat of the oil. Move the aubergine cubes around to ensure that they are cooked on all sides. When they are a deep golden colour all over, remove from the oil and drain on kitchen paper. If needed, add more oil to the pan and heat before frying the next batch. Repeat until they are all evenly cooked.

Add the cooked aubergine chunks to the tomato mixture. Leave to cool and serve at room temperature, as they do in Sicily.

TIP

For *caponata di carciofi*, use artichokes instead of aubergines: either slice fresh artichoke hearts and blanch them, or slice canned ones and add to the mixture.

PATÉ DI MELANZANE
AUBERGINE PÂTÉ

Aubergines can absorb oil with sponge-like ease, but few people look forward to one that is greasy. I first ate this pâté in Spello, a hill town in Umbria, and it is the aubergine's creaminess that is the attraction, with only a small addition of extra-virgin olive oil to finish. The capers add a welcome jab of flavour, but be careful not to overdo the garlic, which can be overwhelming.

Making the pâté is also a great way to make the most of any spare space in the oven when you're baking something else. Note that if your aubergines are watery, and the pâté ends up being rather loose and too liquid to spread, it works very well as a dip. Liven up the colour of the finished pâté with a garnish of finely chopped tomatoes, if you wish.

SERVES 4

Heat the oven to 180°C/160°C fan/gas mark 4.

Put the whole aubergine on a baking tray (as it is, no oil or seasoning). Prick in half a dozen places with a small pointed knife to ensure it doesn't explode and bake in the heated oven for about 50 minutes, until the aubergine is soft when pressed, and the skin is wrinkled. Remove from the oven (take care – it will be very hot) and leave to cool for a few minutes, then remove the skin.

Chop the flesh and put it into a bowl with the garlic, capers, oregano and oil. Season with salt, then blitz with a handheld stick blender to combine. When the mixture is cool, put it in the fridge to chill for at least 1 hour.

When you're ready to serve, stir to mix in any separated liquid, then transfer the pâté to a serving bowl and garnish with a drizzle of oil and the chopped tomatoes, if you wish. Serve with small slices of toast.

1 large aubergine (about 500g)
½ garlic clove, crushed
1 heaped teaspoon capers
a pinch of dried oregano
1 tablespoon extra-virgin olive oil
2 tomatoes, skinned, deseeded and chopped, to garnish (optional)
8 small slices of toasted bread
salt

BISI IN TECIA
PEAS IN A PAN

The farms on the island of Sant'Erasmo in the Venetian lagoon provide much of the produce for the visitor-swamped city of Venice. Visiting a farm there one spring, I was proudly treated to these peas as part of a selection of seasonal *cicchetti* (snacks), served alongside the local *aperitivo*. Their name is local dialect for what is known elsewhere in Italy as *piselli in padella*.

A fresh or grassy-flavoured olive oil works best if you have one, as the focus is on the sunny taste of the peas. These can be served as a starter, or as part of a light lunch alongside a simple salad or a couple of other small plates. Fresh bread makes them easier to handle as an accompaniment to drinks, but you may prefer toast if eating from a plate.

SERVES 4

1 tablespoon extra-virgin olive oil, plus extra to serve
1 small onion, finely chopped
50g carrot, coarsely grated
500g unpodded peas or 200g freshly podded (you could use frozen if necessary)
a few tablespoons hot vegetable stock
8 small slices of bread, to serve
salt and freshly ground black pepper

Heat the oil in a saucepan over a medium heat. Add the onion and carrot, stir to coat, then cook for a few minutes, until the onion is translucent. Add the peas to the pan and stir to mix thoroughly. Cook on a gentle heat for about 20 minutes, stirring every so often and intermittently adding a spoonful of hot vegetable stock to prevent the vegetables from sticking and to help peas to cook. (Be careful not to add too much as you want a dry mixture.) Season to taste with salt and pepper.

When the peas are soft, remove them from the heat and leave to cool. They may well lose their vibrant colour, but they won't lose their flavour.

Place the bread slices on a serving platter, spoon the peas on top and add the lightest drizzle of extra-virgin olive oil before serving.

MILLEFOGLIE DI POLENTA CON PEPERONI
CRISPY POLENTA MILLEFEUILLE WITH PEPPERS

Even people who recoil at the thought of polenta like it cooked this way – crispy and light. The trick is to spread it out thinly, and to work quickly while it is warm and pliable. These millefeuille work well with other veg, such as grilled mushrooms or aubergines, or with tomatoes and vegetarian mozzarella. If you have any left, they will keep for three to four days in an airtight container – try them with dips.

SERVES 4

Blacken the skins of the peppers either by holding them with tongs over a gas flame or by placing on a hot grill pan, turning so that they are charred all over. Place in a bowl and cover with a plate. When cool, remove the stalks, skins and seeds and cut each pepper into 8 strips. Place them on a plate, drizzle with olive oil, sprinkle with salt and pepper and set aside. Heat the oven to 200°C/180°C fan/gas mark 6.

Cook the polenta according to the packet instructions, keeping it slightly looser than usual. Alternatively, add 400ml of water and a generous pinch of salt to a medium-sized pan set over a high heat and bring to the boil. Slowly add the cornmeal in a stream while stirring continuously to avoid lumps forming. Reduce the heat to a simmer and stir frequently using a wooden spoon until cooked (be careful as it is likely to bubble and spit). You may need to add some more hot water should it become too dry or thick; it should be quite loose. Depending on your cornmeal it should be cooked after about 30 minutes. Season well and, using a palette knife, spread the polenta out very thinly (a couple of mm thick) over a large non-stick baking sheet (or use 2 small ones). Don't grease the baking sheet as that will stop the polenta from staying in place. Put the tray in the oven for 10 minutes, until the polenta starts to dry, then remove and reduce the oven temperature to 160°C/140°C fan/gas mark 3.

Using a palette knife carefully lift the polenta from the baking sheet, easing it off gently where it sticks. Turn the polenta sheet over, place it back on the baking sheet and return it to the oven for about 15 minutes, turning it over every 5–7 minutes or so, until it's completely dry and crispy. Remove from the oven, leave to cool and then break it into large pieces and set aside.

Put the vinegar in a small pan over a low heat and add the parsley. Let it infuse for about a minute before removing from the heat. Leave to cool, then whisk in the 6 tablespoons of olive oil to make a dressing.

Alternate layers of polenta and both red and yellow pepper strips. Drizzle over the dressing immediately before serving.

1 red pepper
1 yellow pepper
6 tablespoons extra-virgin olive oil, plus extra for drizzling
100g cornmeal (polenta)
3 tablespoons white wine vinegar
a handful of flat-leaf parsley, finely chopped
salt and freshly ground black pepper

SEDANO MATTO
CRAZY CELERY

A good way to use up an excess of celery, this dish is quick and straightforward to prepare and works well as a starter, or as a light lunch if served with some bread.

It is one of the ways in which celery is served at a casual restaurant in the town of Spoleto. Rungruedee cooks and her husband Filippo Proietti keeps diners entertained at Osteria del Matto, in this beautiful Umbrian town. *Matto* means 'mad' – go there, eat memorably and you'll see just how aptly named the osteria is.

SERVES 4

1 head of celery, sticks separated, de-stringed and cut into 5cm lengths
2–3 tablespoons extra-virgin olive oil
1 large red chilli, chopped
10g vegetarian Italian hard cheese, finely grated, to serve (optional)
salt and freshly ground black pepper

Bring a pan of salted water to the boil and add the celery. Boil for about 2–3 minutes, until the celery is softened but still has some crunch. Drain and pat dry on kitchen paper.

Put the oil and chilli in the pan and cook over a medium heat, until softened but not browned. Add the cooked celery, stir to combine, reduce the heat to medium–low and season with salt and pepper to taste. Leave to warm through for 2–3 minutes, stirring occasionally so that the mixture doesn't catch. Serve sprinkled with grated cheese, if wished.

POLPETTINE DI ZUCCHINE
COURGETTE POLPETTINE

In the small town of Ambivere, to the west of Bergamo in Lombardy, is a family restaurant called Trattoria Visconti. It is civilised and relaxing and, from the outside terrace, diners can glimpse the family's vegetable plot and smile along with the beaming scarecrows who watch over the plants. This dish features on the trattoria's menu when courgettes are at their most plentiful. The inclusion of Amaretti biscuits may be a surprise, but the town of Saronno, from which the liqueur that flavours the biscuits takes its name, is not far away. Add more biscuits if you have a sweeter tooth than I do.

SERVES 4

Pour enough oil into a non-stick frying pan to lightly cover the bottom of it, and warm over a medium heat. Add the shallots to the pan and cook for 5 minutes, until softened, then add the courgettes and cook for 15 minutes, until everything is soft. Leave the courgettes to drain in a colander for 10 minutes, until some liquid runs away and they have cooled slightly. Transfer to a mixing bowl and add the breadcrumbs, cheese, eggs and Amaretti and season with salt to taste. Mix to combine and bring together. Then form the mixture into 16 equally sized patties and lightly dust them all over with flour.

Pour enough oil into a non-stick frying pan to cover the bottom. Place this over a medium heat and, when hot, add the patties a few at a time (take care not to overcrowd the pan). Fry the patties in batches for 3–4 minutes on each side until browned, then remove from the pan and set aside to drain on kitchen paper while you cook the remainder.

Serve hot or cold and sprinkled with the herbs to garnish.

olive oil
2 shallots, chopped
800g courgettes, finely diced
120g dried breadcrumbs
100g vegetarian Italian
    hard cheese, grated
2 eggs, beaten
4 Amaretti biscuits,
    finely crumbled
plain flour, for dusting
a handful of chopped parsley,
    marjoram and chives,
    to garnish
salt and freshly ground
    black pepper

ZUCCA IN AGRODOLCE
SWEET AND SOUR PUMPKIN

The sweet-and-sour union of sugar or honey with vinegar is loved in Sicily, and the addition of fresh mint is a popular way of serving many different vegetables. Enzo Olivieri, originally from Palermo, is a chef who cooks in London and this is his version of a Sicilian classic. It is, by his own admission, 'in-your-face' sour. If you prefer a more even balance of sweet and sour, increase the amount of honey accordingly.

Although this is ready to eat once it is cool, I think it is even better if left until the following day when the flavours have had time to happily settle.

SERVES 4

150–200ml extra-virgin olive oil
500g pumpkin (or butternut
    squash), peeled, deseeded
    and cut into 2cm slices
3 garlic cloves, sliced
a handful of small mint leaves
1 tablespoon runny honey
5 tablespoons white wine vinegar
salt and freshly ground
    black pepper

Place enough of the oil in a large pan to coat the base and place over a medium–high heat. When hot, add the pumpkin slices, reduce the heat to medium–low and fry gently, for about 10 minutes, until soft and browned all over, turning regularly. Transfer the cooked pumpkin slices to a serving dish, season with salt and pepper and set aside while you make the sweet-and-sour sauce.

Add the remaining oil to a pan and add the garlic. Place over a medium–low heat and cook until soft and very lightly golden. Add the mint, honey and vinegar and heat until it is all warmed through.

Pour the sauce over the cooked pumpkin slices and leave to cool before serving.

FUNGHI CARDONCELLI AL FORNO CON CROSTONCINI IN SALSA DI BROCCOLETTI

OVEN-BAKED CARDONCELLI MUSHROOMS WITH BROCCOLI TOASTS

There are two good food reasons to visit the remote town of Orsara di Puglia, in the province of Foggia: the bakery, Pane e Salute, which was established in 1526, and the restaurant Peppe Zullo, owned and run by the eponymous chef. Peppe is an enthusiastic grower of vegetables, fruit and herbs. He is especially ardent about disappearing ancient varieties, and those that are lesser known. For example, *marasciuolo*, which he describes as 'a brassica that has a gentle garlic flavour', is one he uses for this dish. If you can find these leaves, wash them, roughly chop, then leave to marinate in olive oil for at least 15 minutes before using. Otherwise use purple sprouting broccoli and garlic instead (the flavour is a good match) as in this recipe.

SERVES 4

Heat the oven to 200°C/180°C fan/gas mark 6. Put the mushrooms in a baking dish, drizzle with the olive oil and bake for 15–20 minutes, until golden and lightly crisp on the outside.

Meanwhile boil the broccoli and garlic in a pan of salted water for about 5–10 minutes, until well cooked – they should be softer than al dente but not mushy. Drain and cool under very cold running water to set the colour. Pat the broccoli and garlic dry with kitchen paper, then roughly chop and mix them together in a bowl. Add a spoon of olive oil and season with salt and pepper.

When the mushrooms are ready, cut each slice of bread in half and put in the oven for a few minutes to warm through so that the bread becomes slightly crisp without becoming golden. Spoon the broccoli and garlic mixture on to the toasts, place the mushrooms on top and serve with a generous drizzle of olive oil.

500g cardoncelli or chestnut
   mushrooms
3–4 tablespoons extra-virgin
   olive oil
200g purple sprouting broccoli
2 small garlic cloves
4 slices Pugliese bread or
   any rustic bread with
   a crunchy crust
sea salt and freshly ground
   black pepper

RADICCHIO GRIGLIATO
GRILLED RADICCHIO

Treviso radicchio, with its characteristic bitterness, is revered in the area of Venice and the Veneto. The long-leaved *Rossa di Treviso Tardivo* is the elegant super model of this family; it always looks beautifully sculptural and a work of art on the plate. Although I find it delicious served raw in salads, radicchio is more palatable to some after cooking, which diminishes its bitterness. The more compact round varieties are the ones I most usually grill.

Serve this recipe with just a drizzle of oil, or perhaps with a hint of sweet balsamic vinegar. Add chopped hazelnuts, toasted pine nuts or even some vegetarian soft goat's or blue cheese if you wish to make it more of a meal.

SERVES 4

4 radicchio
extra-virgin olive oil, for brushing
    and drizzling
a small handful of flat-leaf
    parsley, chopped
salt and freshly ground
    black pepper

Heat a griddle pan to medium–hot.

Remove and discard any tatty outer leaves from the radicchio. Cut each one in half lengthways and then into wedges, retaining the trimmed root at the bottom as this will hold the leaves together. Lightly brush all over with olive oil, sprinkle with salt and pepper to season, then place each radicchio half cut-side downwards on the heated griddle. Leave for a few minutes until the leaves are tender and the edges char, then turn them over so that the other side cooks.

Serve immediately with a generous drizzle of olive oil and a light sprinkling of parsley.

ASPARAGI E PRIMAVERA
ASPARAGUS AND SPRINGTIME

This is a glorious antipasto for the asparagus season, when the days are becoming brighter and the smell of spring is in the air. At Antichi Sapori in northern Puglia, Pietro Zito uses wild asparagus, which is easily gathered from around the hamlet of Montegrosso where he is based. He also uses new garlic, which has a milder taste than the dried bulbs most of us have to hand.

Pietro uses a *pecorino canestrato* cheese here, which is full-flavoured and tangy. Unfortunately, there are no vegetarian versions of it at present, so if you wish to serve this with cheese, use a vegetarian sheep's milk cheese that can make an impression. He also uses a lot of excellent extra-virgin olive oil and recommends some good-quality bread for soaking it up.

SERVES 4

Combine the oil, garlic and parsley in a wide bowl (to fit the asparagus) and season with salt and pepper. Set aside.

Put enough salted water in a pan to cover the asparagus and add the vinegar. Bring to the boil over a high heat and add the asparagus. Reduce to a simmer and cook for 5 minutes, until tender, then drain. Transfer the asparagus to the bowl with the parsley dressing and make sure they are submerged. Leave to cool and absorb the flavours for a few hours.

To serve, put the asparagus on a plate and pour over the flavoured oil. Sprinkle with black pepper and scatter with cheese shavings if wished. Serve with the hunks of bread for soaking up the oil.

200ml extra-virgin olive oil
4 new garlic cloves or 1 large
    garlic clove, crushed
a large handful of flat-leaf
    parsley, finely chopped
200g wild or regular asparagus,
    trimmed
100ml white wine vinegar
70g medium-strength vegetarian
    hard sheep's cheese, shaved
    (optional)
4 hunks of good-quality bread,
    to serve
salt and freshly ground
    black pepper

PITTULE DI CAVOLFIORE
PITTULE WITH CAULIFLOWER

Pittule are fried balls of dough, known by this and many other names in the Salento, down in the very south of Puglia. They are certainly crowd-pleasers and I've seen people burn their mouths in their rush to eat them straight from the fryer. You'll find them served just as they are, or filled, for example with boiled vegetables. Cauliflower *pittule* are traditionally served on 7 December, the eve of the Feast of the Immaculate Conception.

Monica Olivieri, originally from Lecce, who makes them using this recipe, recommends getting your cat to sleep on top of the bowl to speed up the rising of the dough. She obviously has more luck persuading cats to do things than the rest of us.

SERVES 4

500g type 00 flour, sifted
1 heaped teaspoon active
    dried yeast
375ml warm water
1 small cauliflower,
    broken into florets
olive oil
fig vincotto, to serve (if you can't
    find fig vincotto, any vincotto
    will be suitable)
sea salt

Place the flour in a bowl and make a well in the centre.

Dissolve the yeast in the water and pour the mixture, a little at a time, into the well, mixing it as you go. When all the yeast has been combined, using your hands, mix the dough in the bowl, until it is soft and sticky and will squidge between your fingers (add a little more water if you need to).

Knead it for a further 10 minutes until it is very soft and pliable, then cover the bowl with foil, and a blanket and leave it to rise for about 2–3 hours, depending on how warm your kitchen is, until it has almost doubled in size and has some bubbles.

While the dough is rising, bring a pan of salted water to the boil and add the cauliflower florets. Cook for about 10 minutes, or until al dente. Drain and set aside to cool.

Pour enough oil into a pan to come a third up the sides. Heat until it reaches 180°C on a cooking thermometer.

Wet your hand in cold water, break away a walnut-sized amount of dough and wrap it around a cooked floret, covering it completely. Very carefully place it into the hot oil and fry for about 1–2 minutes, using a long-handled spoon to turn it gently as it cooks, until it is golden on all sides. Remove using a slotted spoon and set aside to drain on kitchen paper. Repeat for the other florets, cooking a few at a time, but taking care not to overload the pan.

Serve while still hot with a sprinkle of salt flakes, and a small dish of fig vincotto for dipping.

BIGOLI

The word *bigoli* usually refers to a long, thick pasta, but not at the restaurant La Stalla, outside of Assisi in Umbria. There, the word is given to a dish that is a longstanding favourite of the clientele: balls of spinach and ricotta cooked in boiling water. As is the case with many Italian recipe names, there is confusion as to why they are so-called. In this case, it was the unexplained choice of the restaurant founders and has become the name that the regulars use, so it is unthinkable that it will be changed now.

I was given a version of this recipe many years ago, one which had no flour in it, and still make mine that way so that they are different from *gnudi*. However, do add a tablespoon of flour if your ricotta is very soft and the bigoli break up.

SERVES 4

Wash the spinach leaves, shake off excess water and put in a pan over a medium heat for about 1 minute, turning the leaves over with a spoon until wilted. Leave to cool slightly. Squeeze the leaves to extract the water and set aside to drain further on kitchen paper, until cool. Then, roughly chop and place in a mixing bowl.

Add the ricotta, eggs and nutmeg to the bowl, season with salt and pepper and mix everything together.

Take about a dessertspoonful of the mixture in your hands and form it into a cocktail-sausage shape. Repeat until you've used all the mixture – it should give you 28–30.

Bring a pan of salted water to the boil. Drop in a few of the bigoli (about 3–4 at a time), taking care not to overcrowd the pan as they need room to move and cook. Rather like gnocchi, the bigoli will sink to the bottom of the pan and then rise to the surface, after about 3–4 minutes, when they are cooked.

Carefully remove the bigoli from the water. They are quite fragile so doing this one by one with a slotted spoon is best. Set each batch aside to drain on kitchen paper while you cook the next. Roll the cooked bigoli in the grated cheese, drizzle over the melted butter and serve immediately.

500g spinach, large
    stalks removed
300g ricotta
2 large eggs, beaten
few gratings of nutmeg
60g vegetarian Italian hard
    cheese, finely grated
80g butter, melted
salt and freshly ground
    black pepper

INSALATA DI ORZO PERLATO
PEARL BARLEY SALAD

Although orzo is commonly thought of as small rice-shaped pasta, it literally means 'barley'; *orzo perlato* is 'pearl barley'. It is a popular grain, especially for soups in the mountainous regions of northern Italy, but this substantial salad is based on one by Patrizia Moretti in Montefalco, Umbria. If you can't find flavourful rocket, peppery watercress works better than bland leaves. Although these quantities provide a good balance of ingredients, feel free to adapt them as you wish.

SERVES 6 GENEROUSLY

350g pearl barley
120g cooked borlotti beans,
    or ½ x 400g can
120g cooked chickpeas, or
    ½ x 400g can
120g cooked fresh or
    frozen peas
about 15 each of green and
    black olives, pitted and sliced
100g rocket, roughly chopped
300g cherry tomatoes, halved
extra-virgin olive oil and your
    choice of vinegar, to serve
salt and freshly ground
    black pepper

Put the pearl barley in a pan of lightly salted water and bring to the boil. Reduce to a simmer and cook for about 40 minutes, until soft but with some resistance. Drain in a colander, then cool under running water and leave to dry.

Mix the beans, chickpeas, peas and olives with the pearl barley. Add the rocket leaves and cherry tomatoes, then season with salt and pepper. To serve, dress with oil and vinegar to taste.

INSALATA DI FAGIOLINI
GREEN BEAN SALAD

My first memory of an Italian green bean salad was in a rustic trattoria in Abruzzo, not far from Chieti. Driving along, we spontaneously stopped for lunch and followed lots of the local workers into their regular place. We entered, were seated and a while later told at breakneck speed what was available that day. But I'd been looking at the other tables and had already made my choice, including the salad. I've since eaten green bean salads all over Italy – often dressed just with oil and lemon juice, but many with this addition of garlic, mint and zest, which I like the best.

SERVES 4

Trim the tops off the beans, then boil them in a pan of salted water for about 5 minutes, until cooked to your liking (I like mine just softer than al dente, but not floppy).

Meanwhile, mix the oil, mint, garlic, lemon juice and zest in a large bowl and season with salt and pepper.

When the beans are ready, drain them and add them to the bowl with the dressing while they're still warm so that they absorb the flavours. Serve warm or at room temperature.

600g French beans
9 tablespoons extra-virgin
  olive oil
a large handful of mint leaves,
  chopped
1 garlic clove, crushed
juice and finely grated zest of
  1 large unwaxed lemon
sea salt and freshly ground
  black pepper

ZUPPA DI FARRO ALL'ARRABBIATA
SPICY FARRO SOUP

I first ate this soup in the town of Orvieto, Umbria, on a damp, wintry day. A big, spicy bowlful, a glass of Sagrantino and some eavesdropping on a heated political discussion at a neighbouring table set us up for a bracing walk around the city and its renowned cathedral. Reliably warming and nourishing when the weather is cold and blustery, this soup is now one I cook regularly.

Soaking the farro for four hours is not essential, but it does reduce the cooking time. If you don't eat this all in one go, the farro continues to absorb the liquid so that it thickens and becomes almost risotto-like.

SERVES 4-6

1 tablespoon olive oil, plus extra
    to serve
½ onion, chopped
1 red chilli, finely chopped
200g semi-pearled farro, soaked
    in cold water for 4 hours
1 litre hot vegetable stock
    or water
1 x 400g can of chopped
    tomatoes
salt and freshly ground
    black pepper

Place the oil in a large pan over a medium heat. When hot, add the onion and chilli and fry, stirring occasionally, for 5 minutes, until softened.

Drain the farro and add this to the pan. Stir to combine. Add half the hot stock or water, bring to the boil, then reduce the heat and simmer for 40 minutes, until the farro has softened somewhat.

Reheat the remaining stock or water and add it to the pan with the tomatoes. Season with salt and pepper to taste. Simmer for a further 20 minutes, until the farro is tender. (Note that farro absorbs a lot of liquid so you may need to add extra hot water from time to time if the soup starts to thicken too much.)

Serve the soup very hot, drizzled generously with extra-virgin olive oil.

MINESTRONE D'INVERNO SALENTINO
SALENTINE WINTER MINESTRONE SOUP

This winter minestrone is perfect for using up small quantities of leftover veg. It is a soup that Monica Olivieri, a food event organiser, used to eat at a friend's house when they were both studying at Lecce university in the Salento area of Puglia. The local recipe includes Leccese chilli powder which she finds too fierce, so she uses French espelette chilli instead. Note that she prefers her vegetable pieces to be quite large, does not believe a minestrone should be served in small portions and uses these quantities for serving two, not four. The Pugliese have impressively healthy appetites.

SERVES 4

Pour the olive oil into a large pan (use as much as necessary to cover its base) and place over a medium heat. When hot, add the leek and cook until softened and starting to turn golden. Add all the other vegetables, stir to combine with the oil and then add the wine. Bring to a simmer and leave for 10 minutes, so that the wine reduces slightly and then add the hot water, or enough to more than cover all the vegetables. Add the salt, cover with a lid and leave to cook on a very gentle heat for 2 hours, until the vegetables are tender and the broth has acquired their flavours. Check the seasoning and adjust if necessary.

Ladle the soup into warmed bowls. Serve with a dusting of the chilli powder, a drizzle of olive oil and slices of toasted wholegrain bread.

200–400ml extra-virgin olive oil, plus extra to serve
½ leek, trimmed, halved and sliced
1 small carrot, trimmed, halved and sliced
½ courgette, trimmed, halved and sliced
½ celery stick, destringed and sliced
180g cherry tomatoes, halved
¼ small butternut squash, peeled, deseeded and cut into about 2cm cubes
100g fresh or frozen peas
2 stems of cavolo nero, leaves stripped and sliced
½ head of cavolo romanesco or cauliflower, separated into small florets and stalks sliced
½ small fennel bulb, cut lengthways and sliced
½ yellow pepper, cut into strips
½ red pepper, cut into strips
2 stems of Swiss chard, thickest part of the stalk removed, then cut into strips
¼ aubergine, cubed
200ml red wine
1 litre hot water
½ teaspoon fine sea salt
espelette chilli powder, to taste
wholegrain bread, to serve

ZUPPA DI FAGIOLINA DEL TRASIMENO
TRASIMENO BEAN SOUP

Trasimeno beans are similar in appearance to black-eyed beans, although a fraction of the size. Back in the 1950s, they nearly disappeared but the tireless efforts of farmers' groups in the area around Lago di Trasimeno in northern Umbria saved them. Now they are protected by a Slow Food Presidium, a protection order for endangered foods. Varying in colour, from pale cream to almost black, with various shades of brown between, these beans do not require soaking, but do wash them thoroughly. If you can't get hold of them, substitute haricot beans or black-eyed beans, and soak them as necessary.

SERVES 4

200g Trasimeno beans, washed
1 large onion, chopped
1 small carrot, peeled
    and finely diced
1 small celery stick,
    destringed and diced
1 garlic clove, crushed
extra-virgin olive oil, for frying
    and drizzling
parsley leaves, chopped,
    to garnish
slices of bread (optional),
    toasted, to serve
salt and freshly ground
    black pepper

Put the beans, half the chopped onion, and all the carrot, celery and garlic in a large pan. Add 1.2 litres of water and place over a high heat. Bring to the boil, then reduce the heat to a simmer and cook for about 45 minutes with the lid partially on, until the beans are almost cooked.

Heat a little oil in a frying pan over a medium heat. Add the remaining onion and fry for a few minutes, until softened and lightly golden.

Add the fried onion to the almost-cooked beans, then bring the mixture back to the boil and cook for a few minutes more, until everything is amalgamated and the beans are tender. Season with salt and pepper to taste.

Ladle the soup into warmed bowls and serve garnished with a sprinkle of chopped parsley, a generous drizzle of extra-virgin olive oil, and a slice of toast per person, if you wish.

ZUPPA CATTIVA DI FAVE
NAUGHTY BROAD BEAN SOUP

This is a straightforward soup made by Carmine Cataldo, a chef in the town of Gerace, in the southern province of Reggio-Calabria. There's nothing *cattivo* or 'naughty' about it, but his restaurant is called Il Lupo Cattivo (The Naughty Wolf) hence the soup's name. I like using fresh (or, out of season, frozen) broad beans for a soup, to make a change from dried ones. Carmine insists on using abundant olive oil – enough to thickly cover the bottom of your pan.

SERVES 4

Heat the olive oil in a pan over a low heat. Add the onion and fry until soft but not coloured. Add the broad beans to the pan and mix everything together. Add the water, increase the heat and bring to a simmer.

Tear the chard leaves into large pieces and lay these on top of the water and beans. Cover the pan with a lid and reduce the heat to very low. Cook for about 30 minutes, until the chard leaves are soft. Season well with salt and pepper to taste. Serve in warmed bowls.

about 100ml extra-virgin olive oil
2 red onions (preferably Tropea), chopped
1kg fresh broad beans, podded; or 300g ready-podded or frozen
1 litre hot water
8 large Swiss chard leaves, stems removed and discarded
salt and freshly ground black pepper

ZUPPA DI LENTICCHIE E CAVOLFIORE

LENTIL AND CAULIFLOWER SOUP

A short distance from the town of Norcia in southern Umbria is the Piano Grande, a big flat plain which, for a very brief period in late spring, is covered in brilliantly coloured wild flowers. As stunning as this is, it is the small hilltop town called Castellucio, perched high on an isolated peak above it, that attracts visitors year round, because it is known worldwide for its lentils – *lenticchie di Castelluccio*.

An intriguing place to walk around, the town has many elderly yet agile residents who cope impressively with the very steep roads. Many sell home-bagged lentils from their front doors to passers by. Be warned, though, that if you choose to buy some from a smiling grandmother, you may well be purchasing the challenge of extracting endless small stones from the lentils. I speak from experience. No matter, their nutty, earthy flavour is revered and they make this gently satisfying soup what it is.

SERVES 4

2 tablespoons extra-virgin olive
   oil, plus extra to serve
2 celery sticks, finely chopped
1 small carrot, finely chopped
1 small onion, finely chopped
2 garlic cloves, finely chopped
1 red chilli, finely chopped
300g cooked Castelluccio
   or other small lentils (about
   160g uncooked)
1 litre good-quality
   vegetable stock
200g cooked cauliflower,
   broken or cut into small florets
   with thicker stalks sliced
garlic-rubbed toast, to serve
   (optional)
salt

Heat the oil in a pan over a low heat. Add the celery, carrot, onion, garlic and chilli. Cook until the vegetables soften but don't colour. Add the lentils and a quarter of the stock. Season with salt, stir to combine and leave to simmer gently for 10–15 minutes to allow the flavours to mingle. Keeping the soup at a gentle simmer, add the cauliflower and cook for a further 5 minutes to heat through. Add the remaining stock and heat through again thoroughly.

Serve just as it is, or with a slice of toast rubbed with garlic and drizzled with oil.

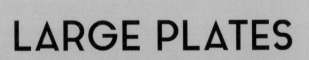

LARGE PLATES

INSALATONA ESTIVA
SUMMER SALAD

In Italian, the suffix -one is added to nouns to convey a large size. For instance, a cat is un gatto, and a large one, un gattone. On a menu, a side salad appears as un'insalata (mista, if a mixed one, or verde if green) in the vegetable or contorni section, whereas large salads appear as insalatone. These large, predominantly seasonal, salads are sometimes served with the ingredients all mixed together, but often with the components separated in individual piles, which I rather like. You'll need to start this recipe an hour or so before you want to serve, to give the ricotta time to drain.

SERVES 4

Wrap the ricotta in a muslin cloth and suspend it (or line a sieve with the muslin and wrap the ricotta inside) over a bowl for up to a couple of hours so that as much liquid as possible drains out of the cheese.

Put the borlotti beans in a bowl and dress with the parsley and oil, salt and pepper to taste.

Heat a griddle pan to medium–hot. Brush the courgette slices on both sides with oil and cook on each side until tender and charred in places. Do this in batches if necessary, and then do the same for the aubergine slices. Set both aside.

Blanch the peas in boiling salted water, then drain and cool under cold running water.

Place the drained ricotta in a bowl. Mix in 1 tablespoon of oil, and two-thirds of the almonds.

Divide the leaves, vegetables and ricotta between 4 serving plates, sprinkling the remaining almonds on the cheese. Season everything with salt and pepper. Drizzle with oil, or with oil and vinegar, if using.

250g ricotta
240g cooked borlotti beans,
    or 1 x 400g can, drained
a handful of flat-leaf parsley,
    chopped
extra-virgin olive oil
2 courgettes, cut lengthways into
    about 5mm slices
1 small aubergine, cut widthways
    into slices
100g podded peas (about 250g
    in their pods)
40g blanched almonds, toasted
    and finely chopped
100g salad leaves, washed
    and torn
12 cherry tomatoes, quartered
1 fennel, cut lengthways into
    8 wedges
red wine vinegar (optional)
salt and freshly ground
    black pepper

INSALATONA CLASSICA
CLASSIC SALAD

Many places have their own house *insalatona* (a main-course salad, as distinct from the *insalata* side). This recipe replicates the 'classic' one from the Met Bar in Terni. I have spent many, many happy hours in this Umbrian town, but it is sadly underrated in guide books. Perhaps that's because it doesn't sit prettily on a hill in a region full of places that do. Although a prosaic, working town, it knows how to party and, just outside, there are some extraordinary, Roman, manmade waterfalls that can be turned on and off. Quirky, perhaps, and in stark contrast to this straightforward and unfussily reliable salad.

SERVES 4

60g lettuce leaves of your choice
a few radicchio leaves
1 large carrot, grated
½ fennel, cored and sliced
   horizontally
24 green olives
12 cherry tomatoes, halved
4 heaped tablespoons
   sweetcorn kernels
8 tablespoons extra-virgin
   olive oil
4 tablespoons red wine
   vinegar (optional)
a few herbs (such as basil leaves),
   to garnish
salt and freshly ground
   black pepper

Divide the vegetables into 4 and arrange them in separate piles on 4 plates. Season with salt and pepper, then dress with olive oil, and the vinegar if you wish. Garnish with herbs, if using, and serve with very good bread on the side.

INSALATA DI PATATE, CIPOLLE ROSSE E UOVA

POTATO, RED ONION AND EGG SALAD

Filippo Cogliandro, a chef in the region of Calabria, recalls this dish from his childhood. He has fond memories of his mother making it in the summer, using potatoes and onions from the garden, and occasionally adding chopped large tomatoes when there was a glut of them. Sweet potatoes aren't often thought of as a southern Italian vegetable, but Filippo explains how they and white potatoes are important in Calabria: 'They were easy to grow and rich in calories for people who needed energy for their physically demanding jobs.'

Tropea is up the coast from Reggio-Calabria. Its eponymous red onions are known for being very sweet, but use other softened red onions, if you can't find a supply of the Calabrians' favourite.

SERVES 4

Cook both types of potatoes in separate pans of boiling salted water until tender enough that when pierced with a knife they fall off easily (approximately 10–12 minutes for the white potatoes and 12–15 minutes for the sweet potatoes). Once cooked, drain and set aside to cool.

Meanwhile, place the slices of onion in a bowl of cold water to soften.

When ready to serve, drain the onions and put them in a bowl with the potatoes and chopped eggs, and mix to combine. Season with salt, dress with olive oil and vinegar to taste and then sprinkle over the cheese.

800g waxy white potatoes, peeled and cut into 2–3cm chunks
400g sweet potatoes, peeled and cut into 2–3cm chunks
2 red onions (ideally Tropea), quartered and thinly sliced
6 hard-boiled eggs, peeled and roughly chopped
50g vegetarian Italian hard cheese, grated
extra-virgin olive oil
red or white wine vinegar
salt

INSALATA INVERNALE
WINTER SALAD

This salad, based on one by Alice Delcourt, chef in Milan, is a lively tasting mixture of winter brightness. Try to use a good assortment of leaves and, if possible, include some deep red radicchio or red chicory, baby kale and head-turning castelfranco. I like some hearty spinach leaves, too; the dressing is not shy and retiring. Do be careful about the quantity of horseradish as there is quite a lot in this dressing. Amend and reduce if you want a less strident flavour, or if your horseradish is particularly fresh and strong. You want it to make its presence felt, but not to overpower the other ingredients.

You'll need to start preparing this dish at least six hours before you intend to cook it.

SERVES 4

200g butternut squash, peeled, deseeded and very thinly sliced with a mandolin or vegetable peeler
at least 300ml red wine vinegar
½ teaspoon salt
1 crisp dessert apple
500g mixed winter leaves

FOR THE SPICY WALNUTS
12g butter
1 tablespoon runny honey
160g walnut halves
smoked paprika, for sprinkling

FOR THE HORSERADISH DRESSING
2 tablespoons lemon juice
1 teaspoon red wine vinegar
1 teaspoon runny honey
20g white miso
½ garlic clove, crushed
20g vegetarian Italian hard cheese, grated
80ml mild olive oil
1 teaspoon salt
½ teaspoon freshly ground black pepper
a pinch of chilli powder or hot paprika
2 tablespoons freshly grated horseradish

Place the squash slices in a flat dish and cover fully with abundant vinegar and salt. Place in the fridge for 5–6 hours.

Prepare the spicy walnuts. Melt the butter and honey together in a small pan over a medium heat. Add the walnut halves, coat with the butter and honey mixture and leave on the heat until golden, stirring to prevent them sticking. Spoon onto a sheet of baking paper. Sprinkle with paprika, season generously with salt and then set aside to cool.

Prepare the dressing. Put all the ingredients in a blender and blitz to combine. Set aside.

Core and thinly slice the apple. Arrange the leaves and apple on a serving platter. Drain the squash, discarding the vinegar, then place it on top of the leaves along with the toasted walnuts. Drizzle over the dressing as liberally as you wish. Serve immediately.

TIP
You'll have some dressing left over, but it usually keeps for a good week stored in the fridge and will liven up winter leaves for other meals.

INSALATA DI RISO
RICE SALAD

For some reason, people have lost appreciation of the rice salad, yet in the Italian summer, from the waterfront in Trieste to the beaches in Puglia, the lunchtime sharing of this easily transportable meal is widespread among families and friends. The idea is a flexible one: long grain rice, with pickles (*giardiniera* is popular, although chopped cornichons or vegetables *sott'aceto* – preserved in vinegar – such as peppers or baby onions will do) and other things that you like. The standard is to add ham or canned tuna, so adjust accordingly and be sure to dress generously. I also like eggs on mine, but leave these and the cheese out should you wish to make a vegan version.

Aside from the essential inclusion of pickles, the other important rule is not to be stingy with the non-rice ingredients. In the blistering sun of an August in Bari, I was once party to an impassioned discussion on whose rice salad was the best. The most scathing criticism arose when there was an excess of rice. The other ingredients should make up at least half your salad.

SERVES 4-6

Cook the rice according to the packet instructions, until tender but retaining a little bite, then drain well.

While the rice is still warm, mix in the pickles, artichokes, olives, capers, sun-dried tomatoes and cheese. Season with salt and pepper and dress with olive oil to taste.

Transfer the salad to a food container, arrange the eggs on top and head to the nearest beach, lake or park to enjoy your picnic. Otherwise, arrange on a plate and serve.

300g long grain rice
500g giardiniera pickles
    (see page 158), drained
8 artichokes in oil, quartered
    (they may come ready-
    quartered)
150g mixed green and black
    olives, pitted
40g capers
100g sun-dried tomatoes in oil,
    roughly chopped
150g mild-flavoured vegetarian
    cheese, cut into small cubes
extra-virgin olive oil, for dressing
4 hard-boiled eggs, shelled and
    quartered
salt and freshly ground
    black pepper

INSALATA DI SPINACI
SPINACH SALAD

In the hamlet of Maggiana on Lake Como, Gabriele Lafranconi runs an osteria called Sali e Tabacchi. He enjoys this salad because 'although it is simple, it combines a balance of elements: the minerality of the spinach, the acidity of the apple and vinegar, the saltiness of the cheese and the fat of the nuts and oil'. As the crow flies, his town of Mandello del Lario is not very far from the Alpine ski resort of St Moritz, but it has a warmer micro-climate than might be expected, and all of the ingredients here are from his home or nearby producers: 'In our garden, among our olive trees, we have a beautiful pomegranate tree that every year gives us a lot of fruit, and oil, apples, walnuts and honey come from producers here on our doorstep.' All these, in a small town to the north of Milan.

SERVES 4

1 slightly unripe Golden Delicious or other eating apple
a squeeze of lemon juice
200g baby spinach
extra-virgin olive oil
apple vinegar
60g walnut halves, chopped
80g pomegranate seeds (seeds from about ½ pomegranate)
160g vegetarian cheese, similar to Quartirolo Lombardo or substitute with vegetarian feta, crumbled
acacia honey, for drizzling
good bread, to serve
salt

Peel, core and cut the apple into slices. Squeeze lemon juice over the slices to prevent them from browning.

Put the spinach in a bowl, dress it with oil and vinegar and season with salt to taste. Scatter the walnuts, pomegranate seeds and cheese over the spinach leaves. Drain the lemon juice from the apple slices and add them to the bowl. Drizzle over some honey and serve with some good bread.

INSALATA DI FARRO AL TARTUFO
FARRO AND TRUFFLE SALAD

This salad is rich with the flavours of Umbrian cooking. Truffles and farro are regional favourites and many families tell delicious tales of truffle-hunting (while staying hand-wavingly vague about their best locations). The meat version of this recipe includes pork sausages, but it is just as satisfying without them. You'll find small jars of mushroom and truffle sauce online or in Italian delis (check the ingredients as some contain non-vegetarian cheese). Although these sauces are mostly mushroom, they have a discernible truffle kick and are full of umami.

If you're lucky enough to have some Umbrian truffles to hand, finish the dish with a light grating. If not, make friends with someone who knows someone...

SERVES 4

Cook the farro in simmering water according to the packet instructions, until softened but with some resistance (usually about 20 minutes). Drain and set aside to cool.

Heat the oil in a pan over a medium heat. Add the mushrooms, season and leave to cook for 10 minutes, until softened and golden brown. Mix in the peas, beans and carrots, then adjust the seasoning, remove from the heat and leave to cool slightly.

Tip the farro into a bowl. Mix in the mushroom and truffle sauce, followed by the cream. Add the vegetable mixture, check for seasoning, then serve topped with a little grated black truffle, if you have it. Leave to cool to room temperature before serving.

250g semi-pearled farro
2–3 tablespoons extra-virgin
   olive oil
250g button mushrooms, sliced
   with stalks
100g fresh or frozen peas,
   cooked
100g fresh or frozen broad
   beans, cooked
100g carrots, diced and cooked
80g mushroom and truffle sauce
75ml single cream
black truffle, to serve (optional)
salt and freshly ground
   black pepper

POMODORO UMBRO
UMBRIAN TOMATOES

Marco Sposino, a chef who works in Tavernelle di Panicale in Umbria, is the inspiration for this dish. He was born and bred in the region and cherishes its tranquillity as well as its food and wine. He's an especially big fan of lentils from Castelluccio, near Norcia and the Piano Grande. They are brown and have an earthy flavour and international renown. If you have any filling left over, enjoy it as a pâté.

SERVES 4

4 large tomatoes
125g Umbrian lentils, preferably
    Castelluccio
about 2 tablespoons extra-virgin
    olive oil, plus extra for drizzling
1 celery stick, thinly sliced
1 small onion, finely chopped
1 small carrot, finely diced
1 garlic clove, crushed
2 large rosemary sprigs, leaves
    picked and finely chopped
salt and freshly ground
    black pepper

Cut off the top fifth of the tomatoes and put to one side. Using a teaspoon, scoop out the central flesh and seeds and reserve. Sprinkle some salt inside the cavity of each tomato. Turn them upside down onto kitchen paper and leave them like that so that their liquid runs out while you prepare the filling.

Bring a pan of salted water to the boil. Add the lentils and cook until al dente (check after 15 minutes and cook a little longer if the lentils are still too hard). Then, remove one third using a slotted spoon and transfer them immediately to a bowl of cold water to stop them cooking. Continue cooking the remaining lentils, checking every 5 minutes or so, until tender.

Heat the olive oil in a separate pan over a low heat. Add the celery, onion, carrot, garlic and rosemary and fry for about 10–15 minutes, until they soften. Chop the flesh from the tomatoes, add to the pan and stir to combine (reserve the tomato liquid if there is a lot of it).

Heat the oven to 200°C/180°C fan/gas mark 6.

Drain the lentils, keeping the cooking water. Add the soft, well-cooked lentils to the cooked vegetables. Season with salt and pepper and blitz with a handheld blender. This mixture should be thick but if it needs loosening, add some of the tomato juice (if you have any) or some of the lentil cooking water. You want the filling to have some texture, so don't make it too smooth. Stir in the al dente lentils.

Put the tomatoes, open ends upwards, in a baking dish and fill each cavity with the lentil and vegetable mixture. Cover with the tomato lids and place in the oven for about 15 minutes, until everything is heated through.

Serve drizzled with a little olive oil and a large green-leaf salad.

PANZANELLA
BREAD SALAD

Italians have numerous ways to use up bread that is past its best, usually in savoury rather than sweet dishes: bread salads for instance, such as *acqua e sale* in Puglia, *salàmoreci* in Sicily or *panzanella* in Tuscany and central Italy. This *panzanella* recipe is based on one by chef Salvatore Denaro. Originally from Sicily, his Umbrian trattoria, with its daily changing menu of irresistible seasonal dishes closed many years ago, but its reputation endures, as does its mythology. He now cooks at the esteemed Arnaldo Caprai winery where he presents an enormous platter of his *panzanella*, beautifully garnished with huge whole basil leaves. Do the same if you are cooking for a large group.

Your bread needs to be quite a coarse bread, and dry, so put it in the oven on a low heat for a short while before using, if necessary.

SERVES 4

Place the bread in a serving bowl. In a jug, combine the vinegar with 250ml of water. Pour just enough liquid onto the bread to dampen it, then squeeze it out and discard any excess liquid so that the bread is softened, but not soaked and mushy. Sprinkle over the salt and white pepper. Add the cherry tomatoes and celery to the bowl, then scatter over the torn basil, olives, oregano, mint and onion or chives. Add abundant extra-virgin olive oil and serve.

4 large coarse, dry bread slices, broken into smallish pieces
50ml white wine vinegar
a very large pinch of salt
a large pinch of white pepper
500g cherry tomatoes, halved
1 celery heart; or 5–6 celery sticks, cut into 2–3cm slices
a large handful of basil, leaves picked and torn, plus a small handful of whole leaves to garnish
250g green olives, pitted
dried oregano, to taste
a large handful of mint leaves, coarsely chopped
1 small onion or a large handful of chives, finely chopped
extra-virgin olive oil

ERBAZZONE
PIE OF MIXED GREENS

Emilia-Romagna has many high-profile culinary specialities, but its vegetarian dishes are less well known. I first ate this pie in the town of Parma, served in thin wedges to accompany *aperitivi*, but it is also enjoyed as a snack or picnic food. It's especially useful for dealing with a glut of Swiss chard or spinach (if you can, use hearty, earthy-tasting spinach rather than baby leaves), or a mixture of both. A thin filling is most usual, but if you prefer a bigger pie, a kilo of leaves gives a good, deep filling.

SERVES 8

FOR THE PIE CRUST
400g plain flour
10g butter, melted, plus extra
   for greasing
3 tablespoons extra-virgin
   olive oil
200ml lukewarm water
salt and freshly ground
   black pepper

FOR THE FILLING
500g–1kg (depending on
   preferred depth) Swiss chard
   and/or spinach, thickest part
   of the stems discarded
100g butter
4 tablespoons extra-virgin
   olive oil
1 garlic clove, peeled
a bunch of spring onions,
   chopped
a handful of parsley leaves,
   chopped
120g vegetarian Italian hard
   cheese, grated
1 egg, beaten
sea salt and freshly ground
   black pepper

Grease a loose-bottomed or springform 26cm tart tin (about 5cm deep if making a bigger pie). Make the dough for the pie crust. In a bowl, mix together the flour, melted butter and olive oil. Season with a generous grinding of salt and pepper, then gradually cut the water into the dry ingredients with a knife. Mix everything together with your hands to form a smooth, elastic dough. Knead this on a lightly floured worktop for a few minutes, then shape into a ball, cover with cling film and leave to rest in a cool place for at least 30 minutes.

Meanwhile, start the filling. Bring a large pan of salted water to the boil and add the chard or spinach. Cook until tender, then drain and leave until cool enough to handle. Squeeze out the leaves to remove as much water as possible, then chop them moderately finely. Squeeze again to remove any remaining water, then lay out to drain on kitchen paper: they need to be as dry as possible to avoid soggy pastry.

Over a low heat, melt the butter in a pan with the oil. Add the whole garlic clove and the chopped spring onions and sweat for about 5–6 minutes, until the onions are softened and the garlic is translucent but not coloured.

Remove the garlic and add the parsley, chard and/or spinach, and season with salt and pepper. Stir to combine and leave on the heat for a few minutes to allow the flavours to mingle. Remove the pan from the heat and leave to cool. Then mix in the grated cheese and set aside.

Heat the oven to 200°C/180°C fan/gas mark 6.

Divide the rested dough into 2 portions (you'll need a slightly bigger one for the pie base). Roll out the larger portion on a lightly floured work surface until big enough to line the prepared tart tin. It doesn't matter if it doesn't quite reach all the way up the sides – it just needs to come higher than the filling so that you can fold over the edges. Spoon in the filling, levelling it as evenly as possible.

Roll out the remaining piece of dough to create a disc to go over the top of the filling. Fold the exposed sides of pastry down over the disc to completely enclose.

Cut a small slit in the top of the pie, then brush it all over with the beaten egg. Sprinkle with salt flakes and bake for 40–45 minutes, until the top is golden brown. Remove from the oven and leave the pie to cool to lukewarm or room temperature before serving.

PANE FRATTAU

Pane frattau is a classic Sardinian dish of the crispiest, wafer-thin bread, layered and topped with tomato sauce, eggs and pecorino cheese. It is filling but frugal. You'll need *pane carasau* for the very thin base, which is sold in many Italian delis and is widely available online. Many years ago, Antonio Carluccio told me that he had used matzo crackers as a substitute and although they work, they make the dish a lot heavier. Many Sardinians use three layers of bread for this; I find that two is substantial enough, but add another if you wish.

SERVES 4

First, prepare the sauce. Heat the oil in a saucepan set over a low heat. Add the garlic and fry gently for a couple of minutes, taking care not to brown. Add the passata and simmer very gently for about 20 minutes, stirring occasionally to ensure that it doesn't stick. Season with salt and pepper and set aside.

Bring a pan of water to the boil (this is for poaching the eggs).

Place a frying pan wide enough to accommodate the sheets of *pane carasau* on a medium heat. Add the stock and when it comes to a simmer, reduce the heat to low so that it stays warm.

Meanwhile, poach the eggs until the whites are set and the yolks are still runny. Remove with a slotted spoon and set aside to drain on kitchen paper until you're ready to assemble.

Put a spoonful of tomato sauce on a serving plate and spread it out. Take 1 slice of *pane carasau* and drop it into the simmering stock. It doesn't matter at all if it's broken (the slices are very fragile so this is likely). Remove it with a fish slice after a couple of seconds as you want it to soften, but not to go mushy or disintegrate. Place this slice on top of the tomato sauce on the plate, then spread some more sauce on the bread layer, sprinkle generously with cheese and then top with another layer of softened *pane carasau*. Finish with another layer of tomato sauce, grated cheese and finally a poached egg.

Assemble the remaining 3 portions and serve immediately.

2 tablespoons extra-virgin
   olive oil
1 garlic clove, crushed
800g passata (see page 159)
500ml vegetable stock
4 large eggs
8 slices *pane carasau*
80–100g vegetarian pecorino
   cheese, grated
salt and freshly ground
   black pepper

FRITTATA COI BOTOI

ARTICHOKE FRITTATA

From mid-April to mid-June, Venetians enjoy small, purple artichokes called *castraure*. They are grown on a handful of islands in the Venetian lagoon and eaten in situ. The Consorzio del Carciofo Violetto di Sant'Erasmo is against producers exporting these local specialities and advises against cooking them. The *castraure* are usually eaten raw, dressed with olive oil and sometimes with Parmesan shavings.

The secondary artichokes, found lower on the plant, are called *botoli* and this frittata is a popular way to eat them. Use the hearts from small artichokes, while in season, or use the ones preserved in oil, adjusting the cooking time accordingly.

SERVES 4

2 tablespoons extra-virgin
    olive oil
1 garlic clove, crushed
½ teaspoon vegetable
    stock powder
8 artichoke hearts, cut into eighths
20g vegetarian Italian hard
    cheese, grated
8 large eggs, beaten
salt and freshly ground
    black pepper

Put the oil, garlic and stock powder in an ovenproof non-stick frying pan with the pieces of artichoke heart. Season with salt and pepper, add a couple of tablespoons of water and place over a medium heat. Cook for 5–6 minutes, turning them over halfway through, until the artichokes are tender.

Meanwhile, in a separate bowl, mix together the cheese and eggs. Heat the grill to high.

When the artichokes are cooked, organise them evenly around the pan in a single layer and pour in the egg and cheese mixture. Leave over a medium heat to allow the eggs to cook for 5 minutes, until the bottom of the frittata has set.

Then, put the frying pan under the grill to cook the top of the frittata for about 2 minutes, until golden or cooked to your liking.

Transfer the frittata to a serving platter and serve hot, cut into wedges.

BROCCOLI STUFATI
BRAISED BROCCOLI

Pietro Zito from Puglia uses *sponsale* onions for this broccoli dish, but I substitute very large spring onions or baby leeks. He also includes caciocavallo cheese but as I haven't yet found a vegetarian version, I use his suggested alternative of breadcrumbs mixed with chopped parsley, salt and pepper, which is traditionally known as 'Parmesan of the poor'. The result, of course, is also vegan.

Milena, who works with Pietro, says that her grandmother used to cook a version of this for her, keeping the broccoli whole and serving it with lots of bread as a *primo piatto*. I find these quantities to be an ample serving for four, but Pietro is a generous feeder.

SERVES 4

Put the broccoli pieces and the leeks or onions into a pan with the tomatoes. Add the parsley and chilli and season with salt and pepper. Pour over 200ml of water and 2–3 tablespoons of olive oil. Cover, put on a medium heat and bring to the simmer. Reduce the heat to very low and simmer very gently for 45 minutes–1 hour, until the broccoli is tender but still a vibrant green colour.

If using breadcrumbs, heat a tablespoon of olive oil in a non-stick pan over a medium heat. Add the breadcrumbs and fry for 2–3 minutes, stirring and turning a couple of times, until golden and crunchy. Mix with the parsley and season with salt and pepper.

Check and adjust the seasoning of the broccoli, then plate up using a slotted spoon. Sprinkle over the cheese or the breadcrumb mixture and finish with a drizzle of oil.

800g–1kg broccoli, florets
 separated and stalks thickly cut
4 baby leeks or very large spring
 onions, quartered lengthways
300g cherry tomatoes
a small bunch of flat-leaf
 parsley, chopped
2 red chillies, finely chopped
about 3–4 tablespoons extra-
 virgin olive oil, plus extra
 to serve
100g vegetarian mature
 cheese, grated; or 100g fresh
 breadcrumbs and a handful of
 chopped flat-leaf parsley
salt and freshly ground
 black pepper

RADICI INVERNALI
WINTER ROOTS

I have not often seen parsnips in Italy, but Cesare Battisti in Milan uses them in his dish of winter root vegetables. Although the idea is straightforward, it does need a good mixture of different types, making it ideal for using up small numbers of veg left behind in the rack. Feel free to include anything that roasts well, even if not root veg, such as squash. The recipe is a fine example of how the Italians use seasonal produce, cooking it at its full-flavoured prime. The final addition of thyme adds a great lift of flavour, and if you have some puréed beetroot to hand, warm it through and add as a dressing.

SERVES 4

800g winter root vegetables
    and tubers, such as celeriac,
    parsnip, Jerusalem artichoke,
    carrot and cooked beetroot
extra-virgin olive oil
few thyme sprigs
salt and freshly ground
    black pepper

Heat the oven to 200°C/180°fan/gas mark 6.

Peel the celeriac, parsnips and any vegetables that can't be cleaned easily. Chop the veg into 2–3cm lengths or cubes and place them together in a bowl. Drizzle over some oil and use your hands to turn the veg until lightly coated. Season with salt and pepper. Tip the vegetables onto a baking tray, add the thyme and bake them for about 20–30 minutes, until cooked through and crisping at the edges.

Arrange the vegetables on a plate and drizzle with oil before serving.

VARIAZIONI DI FINOCCHIO CON LIMONE E CAPPERI

FENNEL VARIATIONS WITH LEMON AND CAPERS

On the edge of the Navigli in Milan is a relaxed restaurant called Erba Brusca. It has a small vegetable garden (*orto*), which enables chef Alice Delcourt to keep closely in touch with the surprises of horticulture, and cook some of my favourite food, using the best produce and serving it beautifully. Half French–half British, she brings influences from her travels and her time at London's River Café and gives an incomer's warm embrace to Italian food. This is a contemporary Italian dish in which each component enhances the others and lets the fennel sing its own unique song.

SERVES 4

First, make the fennel purée. Cut 2 of the large fennel bulbs in half and remove the hardest part of their cores. Slice the fennel very, very thinly, using a mandolin if you have one.

Heat 2 tablespoons of the oil in a large pan over a medium heat. Add the sliced fennel and sauté for about 2–3 minutes, until translucent but not browned. Season with salt and just cover with the stock or water. Cover the pan, reduce the heat to medium–low and allow the fennel to braise gently for about 3–4 minutes, until very tender. With a slotted spoon, transfer to a blender. Purée until very smooth and similar to the consistency of a thick apple sauce, adding a little of the cooking water to loosen if necessary. Once smooth, add the butter and blend again until creamy. Set aside.

Heat the oven to 200°C/180°C fan/gas mark 6.

Take the remaining 2 fennel bulbs and cut each one into 6 wedges. Put them in a roasting tin and rub well with salt and enough oil to coat lightly. Add enough water to cover the bottom of the tin by a few mm and put the fennel in the oven for about 40–50 minutes, until tender and golden. Turn them during cooking when they start to brown.

Meanwhile, make the relish. Set aside some of the fennel fronds for garnish. Chop the other fronds, finely dice the small fennel bulb, and put in a bowl along with the capers, fennel seeds, lemon juice and zest. Add about 1 tablespoon of oil and stir to combine. Taste and adjust the seasoning with salt, if necessary.

To serve, put a generous amount of purée on 4 plates. Arrange 3 roasted fennel wedges on top, spoon over the relish, scatter with the reserved fennel fronds and offer some very good bread.

4 large fennel bulbs, fronds
   removed and set aside
5 tablespoons extra-virgin olive
   oil, plus extra for drizzling
a couple of ladlefuls of hot
   vegetable stock or water
a small knob of butter
1 small fennel bulb
50g drained capers, roughly
   chopped
½ teaspoon toasted and lightly
   ground fennel seeds
juice and finely grated zest
   of 1 unwaxed lemon
salt

INDIVIA CON FAGOTTINO DI PASTA FILLO CON UVETTE, ARANCE E PINOLI

ENDIVE WITH FILO PASTRY PARCELS OF RAISINS, ORANGE AND PINE NUTS

Gabriele Lafranconi, a chef in Mandello del Lario on Lake Como, does not cook with chicory, or what he calls Belgian endive, very often, preferring to use different varieties of radicchio cultivated in the open fields near to him. He usually makes these sorts of parcels in shortcrust pastry (which is more traditional) filled with *radicchio tardivo di Treviso* and locally produced smoked cheese. But, he's happy to ring the changes occasionally.

SERVES 4

4 heads of white endive
  (each about 120g)
4–5 tablespoons extra-virgin
  olive oil
40g raisins
40g pine nuts
30g butter, melted, plus extra
  for greasing
12 sheets of filo pastry, each
  about 15cm square
2 tablespoons balsamic vinegar
1 orange, peeled, pith removed
  and segmented
salt and freshly ground
  black pepper

Remove 8 outer leaves from each head of endive and set aside for the salad. Cut the remaining endives into 2–3cm pieces.

Place a pan over a medium heat. Add 1–2 tablespoons of the oil and, when hot, add the cut pieces of endive. Season with salt and pepper. Add the raisins and half the pine nuts and leave for a few minutes, until the endive is becoming translucent. Remove the pan from the heat and set aside to cool.

Lightly grease 4 tart cases, each about 10cm in diameter, and heat the oven to 200°C/180°C fan/gas mark 6.

Lay out a sheet of filo and lightly brush it with melted butter. Place a second sheet of filo on top at an angle, and brush again. Repeat with a third sheet. Transfer the layered sheets into one of the tart cases so that the edges overhang. Repeat for the remaining filo sheets and cases.

Fill each pastry case with a quarter of the stuffing, then fold the pastry edges over the top to enclose the filling. Brush each parcel with the remaining butter and bake for about 15 minutes, until the pastry is nicely golden.

While the parcels are cooking, toast the remaining pine nuts in a hot, dry frying pan until lightly golden. Set aside. Combine the remaining olive oil with the balsamic vinegar and a pinch of salt to make a dressing.

Place the reserved endive leaves on plates, either whole or coarsely chopped, with the orange segments and toasted pine nuts and drizzle over the dressing. Place the parcels alongside and serve.

SOFFRITTO

A British–Italian friend of mine often asks people, 'What are the three most important vegetables in Italian cooking?'

He says that by far the most usual reply is tomatoes, aubergines and courgettes.

Perhaps this shows what an impression the Mediterranean diet has made on us, or perhaps it's that these three like to take the limelight. If you stop and reflect for a moment, though, you'll soon realise that there is a reason why onions, carrots and celery are often called the 'holy trinity' of *la cucina italiana*. These three, arguably humbler veg, often combined with garlic and parsley, are cooked together at the start of so many dishes – from soups to pasta sauces, via lasagne and lovingly made *sughi*.

While it seems everyone has their own theory about the best way to approach this vegetable foundation, there is general consensus that the 'holy trinity' is indispensable. One point of agreement is that this trio must be cut into small and uniform dice, and many believe that the smaller the dice, the better. Rachel Roddy beautifully describes them as looking like 'vegetable confetti'. I rather enjoy the peeling and fine chopping, but there really is no need to stress if your dice are a little bigger than those prepped in Michelin-starred restaurants.

Avoid using old or past-their-best veg. After all, they are forming the launch pad of your dish so you want them to be fresh and vibrant. You don't want a stale, tired taste to eclipse your other ingredients.

The fat you should cook them in is another matter. Some cooks still stand by the notion of using animal fat (otherwise known as *battuto*), whereas the butter-versus-olive oil divide is far more widespread.

And then there's the question of whether to add garlic or not. There has apparently been an increase in the number of Italians who feel that finely chopped (or any) garlic is misplaced in soffritto (those that a Pugliese friend describes as 'garlicphobes'), whereas I usually welcome it. And what about herbs? Should you include them, or not? Parsley, with its stalks, adds a great freshness of flavour; finely chopped rosemary, woody aromatic notes. Consider the other ingredients in your dish and judge accordingly.

And then to the thorny question of how long to cook a soffritto? A lot of people think that the sweetness of the vegetables comes out only after long, slow cooking – at least an hour on a very low heat. Others think that this is unnecessary and you need a maximum of 15 minutes on a gentle heat (under no circumstances should the garlic be allowed to become brown, or any of the veg to burn). I am in the latter camp.

Whatever camp you find yourself in, though, get the 'holy trinity' cooking, take a look and a smell, and find a method that suits your style. After all, you're building a foundation that supports the food you like.

FUNGHI TRIFOLATI
MUSHROOM TRIFOLATI

Fresh porcini are usually recommended for this dish, but a mixture of wild and cultivated mushrooms is good, or even cultivated mushrooms livened up with some dried porcini (soak 20g of them in hot water for 20 minutes or until reconstituted). This is perfect with Polenta Concia (see page 125), which is quite loose so does not require a sauce. Otherwise, serve the mushrooms on a slice of grilled polenta, or on toasted bread.

My friend Paolo Arrigo, a keen mushroom forager, uses rosemary in his version and says that in his home town of Biella in Piedmont it is believed that only whole garlic cloves should be used because they will turn purple if there is a toxic mushroom in the pan. I wouldn't rely on that method, but do leave the garlic intact so that it can be discarded after gently flavouring everything, if you prefer.

SERVES 4

Chop the mushrooms into slices or chunks or leave whole, depending on their size. Heat the oil and butter in a pan over a medium–high heat. Add the garlic and mushrooms. Season with salt and pepper and cook, stirring occasionally to prevent catching, for about 10 minutes, until the mushrooms are tender and their moisture has evaporated. Sprinkle over the parsley and serve.

400g mixed mushrooms
4 tablespoons mild olive oil
30g butter
1 large garlic clove, crushed
a handful of flat-leaf parsley, chopped
salt and freshly ground black pepper

COCOTTE DI SEDANO RAPA CON PATATA E FORMAGGIO VERDE

CELERIAC, POTATO AND BLUE CHEESE PIE

The southern band of Lombardy, home to the rich agricultural plain of the Po River, is often called the 'white belt' owing to its production of rice, cheese and butter. In the hamlet of Grazie di Curtatone, on the outskirts of the city of Mantova, is Fernando Aldighieri's family trattoria, where you'll find the idea for these pies. They are substantial and filling, but then Fernando likes his guests to depart happy and with full bellies. Season generously, as the potatoes, celeriac and pastry mute the flavours of the blue cheese.

SERVES 4

900g floury potatoes, peeled and cut into medium-sized pieces
2 small celeriacs (about 750g each), peeled and each cut into at least 6 slices of 5mm
100ml single cream
250g vegetarian strong-flavoured blue cheese
butter, for greasing
250g puff pastry
1 egg, beaten
salt and freshly ground black pepper

Boil the potatoes in salted water until tender, then drain, mash and season. While the potatoes are cooking, boil the celeriac slices in salted water until tender, then drain them and lay them on kitchen paper to dry out.

Place the cream in a pan over a gentle heat. Cut the cheese into large cubes and add to the pan. Allow the cheese to melt, then taste, season, and mix in thoroughly with the mashed potatoes.

Lightly grease 4 ovenproof bowls or mini casserole dishes with butter. Put the celeriac in the bottom of each dish (you may need to cut them and layer the pieces to fit), then add a layer of cheese and potato. Repeat at least twice more, until you've used all the celeriac and cheesy mash.

Heat the oven to 200°C/180°C fan/gas mark 6.

Roll out the puff pastry large enough so that you can cut a lid for each dish (re-roll if necessary). Top each pie with a pastry lid and make a cut, or two, in the centre. Brush with beaten egg.

Bake the pies for 20 minutes, until golden, then serve piping hot with steamed green vegetables if wished.

PARMIGIANA DI MELANZANE
AUBERGINE PARMIGIANA

I got to know Salvatore Denaro at his erstwhile trattoria, Il Bacco Felice, in Foligno, Umbria, where he had a deserved reputation for excellent food and spirited hospitality. Alas, Il Bacco Felice is no more, but this parmigiana is based on one of Salvo's recipes. Whereas usually the layers of aubergine, tomato and cheese are assembled in a baking dish and finished in the oven, this version uses tomato slices and is simply heated through in a frying pan to serve warm rather than piping hot. It is an ideal option for the summer months.

The word *parmigiana* refers not to the cheese, but to shutters and the way in which the slices of aubergine are layered. So, whether your version includes true Parmigiano Reggiano or a vegetarian substitute, this is still the right name.

SERVES 6

Salt the aubergine slices and leave them for 30–40 minutes to draw out the juices. Thoroughly wipe them dry, then brush them with oil.

Heat a large, non-stick frying pan over a medium heat. Add the aubergine slices and fry in batches for 2–3 minutes on each side, until cooked and golden. Set aside on kitchen paper to drain off the excess fat.

Wipe the pan clean and, off the heat, cover the bottom of it with the breadcrumbs. Take half of the aubergine slices and layer them on the breadcrumbs, then lay over all of the tomato slices and season with salt and pepper. Cover with the torn basil, then grate over the cheese and cover with the chopped eggs. Finally, layer over the remaining aubergine slices. Heat the parmigiana on a medium–low heat for about 10 minutes, until the breadcrumbs are crispy.

To serve, either take the dramatic route of putting a serving dish over the frying pan and inverting the contents on to it, or simply cut individual slices from the pan, inverting as you serve so that the breadcrumbs are on the top.

When the weather is very hot, you can refrigerate the parmigiana for a couple of hours, but it is best served neither too hot nor too cold.

2 large aubergines, sliced
    into rounds approximately
    1cm thick
extra-virgin olive oil, for brushing
50g dried breadcrumbs,
    seasoned with salt and pepper
300g tomatoes, sliced
    4–5mm thick
a large handful of basil leaves,
    roughly torn
50g vegetarian Italian
    hard cheese
3 hard-boiled eggs, peeled and
    very roughly chopped
salt and freshly ground
    black pepper

FARROTTO CON FAGIOLINI, ZUCCHINI, PATATE E PESTO

FARROTTO WITH GREEN BEANS, COURGETTES, POTATOES AND PESTO

Eaten in Italy since antiquity, farro was the grain that fuelled the Roman armies. It has become popular again and I like to use it in a *farrotto*, where it replaces the rice of a risotto. This recipe is the first *farrotto* I cooked regularly at home and it remains an easy standby. It also works with cubes of roasted squash instead of potato, or strips of grilled green peppers instead of the beans. I've been known to use a tarragon pesto for a change, but the original with Pesto Genovese (page 162) remains my first choice. Note that the farro will cook more quickly if you soak it in cold water for a couple of hours first.

SERVES 4

100g green beans, cut into
    2–3cm pieces
100g courgettes (about ½
    courgette), diced
100g waxy potatoes (such as
    Charlotte), cut into small cubes
2 tablespoons extra-virgin olive
    oil, plus extra for finishing
200g pearled or semi-pearled
    farro or spelt, soaked and
    drained
500ml hot vegetable stock
2 generous tablespoons basil
    pesto (see page 162)
vegetarian Italian hard cheese,
    shaved, to taste
salt and freshly ground
    black pepper

Bring 3 pans of salted water to the boil. Add the beans, courgettes and potatoes each to a pan and cook until al dente. This will take about 2–4 minutes for the beans, 1 minute for the courgettes and 4–5 minutes for the potatoes, but be guided by how you like them cooked. (Cooking separately ensures they retain their individual flavours.)

Heat the olive oil in a separate pan over a gentle heat. Add the farro or spelt and stir to coat it in the oil. Add the stock a ladleful at a time, stirring the grains and waiting until the liquid has been absorbed before adding the next ladleful as you would when making a risotto. Note that farro is quite forgiving, so it's not necessary to stir it relentlessly; you can leave it momentarily, if you like. The whole process should take about 15 minutes (but the exact time will depend on how long you soaked the farro before beginning), until the farro is cooked but still chewy.

Add the beans, courgettes and potatoes. Season to taste with salt and pepper and stir to combine and heat through the vegetables. Finally, mix in the pesto.

Serve with the grated cheese and a generous drizzle of extra-virgin olive oil.

GNUDI DI RICOTTA CON ZUCCHINI
RICOTTA GNUDI WITH COURGETTES

The first time I came across *gnudi* or 'naked ravioli' was at a restaurant in Chiusi, Tuscany. The chef described them as 'the filling without the clothes'. You can make these with gram flour, but I prefer the more delicate result that wheat flour gives. Use the best ricotta you can find; often supermarket options are watery, so let those sit on muslin to drain away any excess liquid, if necessary. These *gnudi* are very good with just melted butter and grated cheese if you want to keep them simple.

The *gnudi* are a little bit fiddly to make at first, but with practice you'll find them mesmerisingly therapeutic, and they're always a dream to eat. It helps if your kitchen is cool, but either way you'll need to leave time for the *gnudi* to firm up so make them early in the morning and leave them to chill, or make them the day before and leave them in the fridge overnight.

SERVES 4

FOR THE GNUDI
250g ricotta
2 egg yolks
100g vegetarian Italian hard
    cheese, grated, plus extra
    to serve
finely grated zest of
    1 unwaxed lemon
20g plain flour, plus extra
    for coating
salt and freshly ground
    black pepper

FOR THE SAUCE
1 courgette, trimmed and halved
    lengthways
120g vegetarian soft
    goat's cheese
2 tablespoons white wine,
    plus an extra splash
2 tablespoons extra-virgin olive
    oil, plus extra to serve
1 large garlic clove, peeled then
    left whole
a handful of shredded basil or
    marjoram, plus extra to garnish

In a bowl, mix all the *gnudi* ingredients together to a smooth paste.

Dust your work surface with flour, and have to hand a small bowl of cold water (wet fingers make the rolling easier). Take a heaped teaspoon of the mixture, form it into a ball in your hands, then, roll it in the flour to give a thin coating. Set aside and repeat until you have about 20 *gnudi*. Cover and chill in the fridge for a good few hours or overnight. This settling and chilling time is important.

Just before you cook the *gnudi*, make the sauce. Take the courgette halves, scoop out the seedy centre and discard, then dice the flesh very finely. In a small bowl, combine the goat's cheese with the white wine. Set both aside.

Heat the oil in a saucepan over a low heat. Add the garlic and leave to infuse the oil for a few minutes, until the clove starts to change colour. Remove and discard the clove, then add the diced courgette, then the basil or marjoram. When the courgette has softened (about 3–4 minutes), add the splash of white wine and remove the pan from the heat. Stir in the cheese and wine mixture and season with salt and pepper to taste. Return the pan to a very low heat to keep warm.

Bring a pan of salted water to the boil. Gently add the *gnudi* and cook for about 4–5 minutes, or until they rise to the surface of the water. Remove them with a slotted spoon and leave to drain on kitchen paper.

Spoon the sauce onto 4 serving plates and divide the *gnudi* between them. Sprinkle with grated cheese and the shredded basil, and finish with a drizzle of extra-virgin olive oil.

BRUSTENGO DI PATATE E CAVOLO
POTATO AND CABBAGE BRUSTENGO

This Umbrian dish is like an Italian version of the British bubble and squeak. Apparently, it used to be served as an antipasto, but I've only ever seen it as a vegetable dish. You can, of course, vary the quantities: increase or decrease the ratio of potato to cabbage depending on your mood or what you have. I like mine with the garlic making its presence felt, but if you prefer a more delicate taste, just flavour the oil with a garlic clove and then discard it. Is 'brustengo' or 'bubble and squeak' the better name? I like them both.

SERVES 4

Bring a large pan of salted water to the boil and add the potatoes. Cook for about 15–20 minutes, or until tender enough to mash (precise cooking time will depend on how small you chop them). Meanwhile, bring a second pan of salted water to the boil and cook the cabbage for about 4–5 minutes, until tender. Drain both thoroughly.

Mash the potatoes well, then season and add some olive oil if you like. Add the cabbage to the mashed potato, stir to combine and season with salt and pepper.

Heat the oil in a large, non-stick frying pan over a low heat. Add the garlic and gently fry for about 1 minute, until softened. Then, add the potato mixture to the frying pan, combine with the cooked garlic and flatten it with a wooden spoon to give a frittata shape. Increase the heat to medium and fry for about 7 minutes, until the underside is nicely browned. Invert the brustengo onto a plate, then slide it back into the pan to cook for a further 3–4 minutes to brown the other side.

Serve hot in slices.

800g floury potatoes, peeled and cut into large pieces
500g savoy cabbage, cored and shredded
4 tablespoons extra-virgin olive oil, plus extra for mashing if you like
2 garlic cloves, crushed
salt and freshly ground black pepper

GNOCCHI DI PATATE RIPIENI DI FUNGHI
MUSHROOM-FILLED POTATO GNOCCHI

Gnocchi stuffed with minced meat are found in various regions of Italy, and the idea works well with mushrooms. I use Désirée potatoes, as they hold together well without the need for too much flour (which can make gnocchi claggy and unpleasant). Chop your mushrooms very finely as this will make the parcels easier to form, and make sure your filling is as dry as possible to prevent them becoming soggy (the drained mushroom liquid adds great flavour to the melted butter).

SERVES 2-4 DEPENDING ON HUNGER

FOR THE MUSHROOM FILLING
2 tablespoons extra-virgin olive oil
180g mixed mushrooms, very finely chopped
1 garlic clove, crushed
a small handful of thyme leaves
salt and freshly ground black pepper

FOR THE GNOCCHI
450g potatoes (such as Désirée), peeled and cut into pieces
85g plain flour
a splash of extra-virgin olive oil
120g butter
a handful of sage leaves

First, make the filling. Heat the oil in a pan over a low heat. Add the mushrooms, garlic and thyme, season to taste with salt and pepper and cook for 4–5 minutes, until the mushrooms are browned and have released their liquid. Tip them into a sieve set over a bowl to drain and leave to cool. Reserve the liquid.

Meanwhile, make the gnocchi. Boil the potatoes in salted water until tender. Drain them thoroughly, then pass through a potato ricer, or mash them until they are smooth and creamy with no lumps. Season with salt and pepper.

Mix the flour into the warm potatoes. Tip out the mixture onto a very lightly floured surface (you want to add as little extra flour as possible) and knead together to form a dough. Roll out to about 4mm thick with a rolling pin, and using an 8cm pastry cutter or the equivalent rim of a glass, cut out discs, re-rolling the dough when necessary. You should have about 20.

Place a small amount of the mushroom mixture onto each disc and then gather up the edges over the filling and press together to form balls.

Bring a saucepan of salted water to the boil. Add the gnocchi a few at a time and leave for 4–6 minutes, until you have cooked out the flour and they are heated through (they will rise to the surface when ready, but the boiling water can throw them around making it hard to tell). Remove them gently one by one, with a slotted spoon, and set aside to drain on kitchen paper.

Heat the splash of oil in a non-stick pan over a medium heat. Add the drained gnocchi and cook in batches for 3–4 minutes, turning very gently until browned on all sides.

In a separate pan melt the butter (let it caramelise slightly) with the sage leaves and add the reserved mushroom liquid to form a sauce.

Divide the gnocchi equally between 4 plates. Spoon over the flavoured sauce and sage leaves and serve immediately.

RISOTTO DI CAVOLO NERO
TUSCAN KALE RISOTTO

There are countless discussions to be had with Italians about *risotti*: there's the choice of rice (arborio versus carnoroli versus vialone nano); the *mantecatura* (the final addition of butter and perhaps cheese); the necessity of continuous stirring. Many a risotto includes pieces of chopped vegetables. Fair enough, but there is also the option of using puréed veg, which means you can include a lot more vegetable. Alice Delcourt cooks this recipe in her restaurant Erba Brusca in Milan.

SERVES 4

Toast the hazelnuts in a small frying pan over a medium heat for about 3 minutes until they become lightly golden. Roughly chop and set aside.

Bring a pan of salted water to the boil. Add the kale leaves and cook for about 5 minutes, until tender. Drain and run under cold water to set the colour, then transfer the wet leaves to a blender and blitz to a smooth purée. Set aside.

Put your stock in a pan, heat it through and keep it gently simmering on a medium–low heat.

Add the olive oil to a pan and place over a low heat. Add the onion and sauté for 4–5 minutes, until translucent. Increase the heat to medium, add the rice and stir to coat in the onion and oil, then add a few ladlefuls of the hot stock. Allow the rice to absorb the stock, stirring often, then add another few ladlefuls of stock. Keep going until the rice is still crisp inside, but starting to soften on the outside (you may not need all the stock).

Add the kale purée, stir and heat through, then test the rice – if it still has too much bite, add further ladlefuls of stock until the rice is cooked, allowing it to absorb the stock each time before adding the next. Season to taste with salt and pepper, bearing in mind that the cheese will add saltiness, too. Stir in half the lemon zest and all the lemon juice.

Remove the pan from the heat. Stir in the butter and cheese until melted and the rice looks creamy. Serve immediately garnished with the chopped hazelnuts and the remaining lemon zest.

60g blanched hazelnuts
400g Tuscan kale (cavolo nero), leaves torn from the ribs
1.5 litres vegetable stock
a splash of extra-virgin olive oil
½ onion, finely chopped
400g carnaroli rice
finely grated zest of 2 unwaxed lemons and juice of 1
50g butter
50g vegetarian Italian hard cheese, finely grated
salt and freshly ground black pepper

RICE

It is impossible to think of Italian food without risotto, the country's celebrated rice dish. But rice is used in many other ways too – in soups (such as *ris e verz*, or rice and cabbage) and minestrone, for stuffing vegetables (see the cabbage involtini on page 121), for salads (see the rice salad on page 71) and as a side dish (often plain boiled rice with butter).

Venice has its well-known rice and peas, *risi e bisi*, Piedmont its *paniscia* and Milan its *risotto alla Milanese* or *risotto giallo*, made with saffron (Gualtiero Marchesi, the late deified chef, added a large square of gold leaf to his). In the south, Sicilians (and increasingly many around the world) enjoy fried rice balls in the form of arancini. If you like them, try *supplì al telefono*, which are filled with cheese that is said to resemble phone cords when it softens and forms strings.

The Italians extensively export the widely grown varieties of carnoroli, vialone nano and arborio rice. Although large companies mostly now grow and process the country's rice crops, there remain smaller growers and many of these still sell their grains to rice mills that have been in the same family for generations. For example, Riseria Schiavi in Castiglione Mantovano di Roverbella, in Lombardy, was founded in 1687 and still uses a mill dating from before 1900.

If you want to find the most inspiring and interesting rice recipes, head to the northern regions of Piedmont, Lombardy and the Veneto. It's no coincidence that these are where most rice is grown. The Po Valley, for example, has the right conditions for cultivation of the grain, making paddy fields a significant part of the verdant landscape and *risotti* a dietary staple of its residents.

POLENTA

Polenta has long been a staple food in northern Italy and although the word can mean any mix of ground cereal with water, these days it generally refers to maize. Most usually the colour of yellow corn, there is also a white polenta, seen in regions such as Friuli-Venezia-Giulia and the Veneto, which is made from white maize and is more delicately flavoured. For a gutsier taste, head to the Valtellina in Lombardy for a version made from a mix of maize and buckwheat.

Traditionally, polenta has taken muscle power to make, being stirred continuously (convention says this should be done clockwise) with a long-handled, wooden spoon in a large copper pan called a *paiolo*. It is now easy to find electric paddle saucepans that do the stirring for you. They are indispensable in many a professional kitchen.

Polenta is versatile and can be served soft or 'wet' (making it with milk rather than water results in a creamier polenta, and those who prefer it to be looser simply add more liquid). Or, once it is cooked, you can spread it out on a baking tray until it solidifies, then cut it into slabs and grill it or heat it in a griddle pan. Alternatively, cut it into small pieces and fry to make polenta chips. Otherwise, spread it out very thinly while it's still wet and then dry it out in the oven to make crisps (see page 29).

Although classically served alongside meat braises and stews, polenta does take on the flavour of whatever you serve it with, so works very well with vegetables such as mushrooms (see page 97).

However it is made, generous seasoning is key. And, understandably, versions with added cheese, such as Polenta Concia (page 125) or *polenta taragna*, remain popular, classic comfort food.

RISOTTO ALLE RAPE ROSSE E TOPINAMBUR
BEETROOT RISOTTO WITH JERUSALEM ARTICHOKES

Cesare Battisti serves this beautifully coloured dish at his restaurant, Ratanà, in Milan. He's such an acclaimed risotto maker that he was named the Rice Ambassador for Milan's Expo 2015. In a region where rice is revered, that is recognition to be taken seriously.

For the *mantecatura* (the end of the risotto making when butter, and cheese if appropriate, is beaten into the rice with a wooden spoon to make it creamy), Cesare uses top-quality mountain butter and 24-month matured Lodigiano cheese. Use the best butter you can – although you may wish to use less than suggested here – and note that it does cool down the rice quite rapidly, so be ready to serve straight away.

SERVES 4

2 large beetroots
about 1 litre vegetable stock
  (see Tip)
3 tablespoons extra-virgin olive
  oil, plus extra for frying the
  Jerusalem artichokes
1 small onion, halved
240g carnaroli rice
2 Jerusalem artichokes,
  washed and thinly sliced
  with a mandolin
80g butter
60g vegetarian Italian hard
  cheese, grated
a handful of cress

Cook the beetroots in lightly salted simmering water for 2 hours, until tender. Leave to cool in the water, then peel them and purée them in a blender. Set aside. (While the beetroots are cooking is a good time to make your vegetable stock; see Tip, below.)

Put your stock in a pan, heat it through and keep it gently simmering on a medium–low heat. Place the olive oil in a large pan over a medium heat and when hot, add the onion and the rice. Cook for about 5 minutes, stirring. Remove the onion when it browns. When the rice becomes translucent, start adding the hot vegetable stock, one small ladleful at a time, stirring the rice continuously as you do so and adding the next ladleful after the previous one has been absorbed. After 10 minutes, add the warmed beetroot purée and continue cooking the rice, adding the stock a ladleful at a time, and stirring until it is tender with the amount of bite that you like. Shortly before it is ready, prepare the artichokes.

In a frying pan, fry the Jerusalem artichoke slices in olive oil to give golden crisps. Set them aside to drain on kitchen paper.

Remove the rice pan from the heat; stir in the butter, then the cheese. Arrange the risotto on 4 plates and decorate with the artichoke crisps and a few snips of the cress. Serve immediately.

TIP
The vegetable stock needed for this recipe is easy to make. Add the following to a pan with 1.5 litres of water, bring to the boil and simmer for 1–1½ hours, season and strain: 1 carrot, peeled and quartered; 1 celery stick, quartered; 1 small onion, quartered; 1 leek, quartered; 1 bay leaf; 1 tomato, quartered.

INVOLTINI DI VERZA RIPIENI DI RISO E LENTICCHIE AL POMODORO

SAVOY CABBAGE ROLLS WITH RICE AND LENTILS

Stuffed cabbage is a familiar lunch in Lombardy, albeit traditionally with a meat filling. But the concept is well-loved so chef Gabriele Lafranconi in Mandello del Lario makes a rice-and-lentil version for his vegetarian diners.

I add garlic and shallots to the rice and lentil mixture for a bit more flavour, and you could also add some chilli or other spices – treat the base as a blank canvas. I find the involtini enough by themselves but they are often served hot, with wet polenta or grilled polenta slices alongside.

SERVES 4

In two separate pans of salted water, cook the lentils with the bay leaf in one, and the rice in the other, both according to the packet instructions.

Meanwhile, heat half the olive oil in a pan. Fry the garlic and half the chopped shallots over a medium heat for about 5 minutes, until the shallots are golden. Set aside. When the rice and lentils are cooked, drain them and leave to cool, discarding the bay leaf.

Remove the hardest part of the rib from the cabbage leaves, then add them to a pan of boiling salted water and boil for about 3–4 minutes, until tender. Transfer to a bowl of cold, salted water to cool, then drain and dry them with a clean tea towel.

In a bowl mix together the lentils and rice with the cooked shallot and garlic. Season generously with salt and pepper.

Heat the remaining oil in a pan over a medium heat. Add the remaining shallot and cook for about 5 minutes, until golden. Add the passata and stir and heat through to make a light sauce.

Heat the oven to 200°C/180°C fan/gas mark 6.

Spread out a cabbage leaf. Bring one eighth of the rice and lentil mixture together in your hands and place in the centre of the leaf. Roll the leaf around and fold the ends under to enclose the mixture, turning it over so that the folded side is on the bottom and the parcel stays put. Repeat for the remaining mixture and leaves.

Pour the tomato sauce into a baking dish and lay the cabbage rolls on top. Bake for about 15 minutes so that everything is heated through. Serve with polenta, if you wish (see recipe introduction).

100g Italian brown lentils
1 bay leaf
100g rice (any type)
4 tablespoons extra-virgin olive oil
1 garlic clove, crushed
2 shallots, finely chopped
8 large Savoy cabbage leaves
500g passata (see page 159)
salt and freshly ground black pepper

FINOCCHI ARRAGANATI ALLA VECCHIA MANIERA

OLD-STYLE FENNEL GRATIN

Pugliese fennel are deliciously full-flavoured. Pietro Zito in Montegrosso serves them, as well as his other bountiful crops, in all sorts of ways at his brilliant restaurant, Antichi Sapori. Not many of us have the vegetables that Pietro has to hand in our own homes but we can follow his example of using the best fresh produce and cooking it simply. For this dish, Pietro uses winter cherry tomatoes, locally produced pecorino cheese and a clay pot. However, we can make do with regular cherry tomatoes, the best vegetarian pecorino we can find and a conventional baking dish. Search out large fennel, because big, wide bulbs work best.

SERVES 4

2 large fennel, trimmed and
    halved lengthways
about 1 tablespoon extra-virgin
    olive oil
50g dried breadcrumbs
20g vegetarian pecorino,
    finely grated
a handful of parsley,
    finely chopped
1 red chilli, finely chopped
250g cherry tomatoes,
    finely chopped
200ml warm water
salt

Heat the oven to 200°C/180°C fan/gas mark 6.

Rub the fennel halves lightly with some olive oil and sprinkle with a little salt. Put in a baking dish, then into the oven for 20 minutes until partially softened.

Meanwhile, in a bowl mix together the breadcrumbs, cheese, parsley and chilli and season with salt. Pour in enough olive oil to hold the mixture together. Set aside.

Take the fennel bulbs from the oven and top them with a layer of chopped tomatoes, followed by the breadcrumb mixture.

Pour the warm water into the bottom of the baking dish, taking care to avoid making the breadcrumbs wet. Bake for a further 20–30 minutes, until the fennel is tender and the topping is bubbling and golden. Remove from the oven and serve immediately.

POLENTA CONCIA

This is a rich, warming and filling dish from Biella in Piedmont. Paolo Arrigo, whose family comes from the town, claims that 'you should always eat polenta when the weather's cold' and that only a wooden spoon will do for the stirring (ideally in a copper pot – but a conventional pan will do). He also explains that the melted cheese should form strings when you ladle it out – so choose a vegetarian cheese that will melt in that way. Finally, some say that you should avoid cold drinks when eating *polenta concia* unless you want indigestion or a heart attack. Be warned.

SERVES 4

Put 500ml of water in a pan and add the salt and the milk. Place over a high heat and bring to the boil. Add the knob of butter, then slowly add the cornmeal in a stream, stirring continuously to prevent lumps. Reduce the heat and simmer according to the packet instructions, stirring occasionally, until cooked (when it starts to come away from the sides of the pan). Add more hot water if at any point it looks too thick or dry. Set aside and keep warm.

In a separate pan, heat the 100g of butter and the sage leaves over a medium heat for about 3–4 minutes, until the butter is lightly browned and the sage is crispy, but be careful not to burn.

Just before serving, return the polenta to a medium heat, add the cheese pieces and stir thoroughly to ensure that all the cheese is mixed in and melted. Dish up into warmed bowls, pour some of the melted, flavoured butter onto each portion, share out the sage leaves, and season with some freshly ground black pepper.

1 tablespoon salt
1 litre whole milk
100g unsalted butter, plus an extra knob
500g cornmeal (polenta)
200g cheese (a mix of 2 hard, vegetarian mountain cheeses, similar to toma or fontina)
a generous handful of large sage leaves
freshly ground black pepper

PASTA

Pasta is one of Italy's quintessential foods. It is popular worldwide and the demand for it is huge. All very impressive for a foodstuff that can easily be made from merely water, flour and salt. There are records of it being eaten back in Roman times, and the story of Marco Polo bringing it to Europe from China is now widely acknowledged to be wrong.

The oft-held belief that fresh pasta is better than dried is also wrong. An Italian friend in Puglia talks frequently about the advantages of dried pasta: the cooking time isn't as sensitive as with fresh pasta, and it has the benefit of an al dente centre. In short, a commercially and well-made dried pasta is preferable to a badly made fresh one.

Although making pasta at home is easier when using a machine, having one is not essential. Many Italians use a *mattarallo*, a rolling pin – albeit often a very long one – for making sheets of pasta, whether at home or in restaurants. Where homemade egg pasta really comes into its own is when you want to make stuffed pastas, ravioli, tortelloni, pansotti and so on, complete with your own fillings. Serve these with melted butter, a light sauce or in vegetable broth.

There are hundreds of different pasta shapes throughout the country, many with charming names, such as *cavatappi* (corkscrews), *fazzoletti* (handkerchiefs), *maltagliati* (badly cut), *ditali* (thimbles) and *cappelletti* (little hats). Whatever the shape, your pasta needs cooking in a large pan, with copious salted water (the recipe for Cacio e Pepe on page 141 explains why the cooking method for this pasta dish is an exception).

If you need to be precise about pasta (as we know and love it), then the term '*pasta alimentare*' is the one to use. This is to differentiate it from other pastes and doughs also called 'pasta', as well as the fact that *una pasta* is a pastry.

Don't forget that pasta, traditionally served as the primo course in an Italian meal, should not be swamped in sauce. There is, after all, substantial food to follow, and the pasta itself should be good enough to let its own taste shine.

EGG PASTA

**MAKES ENOUGH FOR
4-5 PEOPLE**

Sift the flour into a bowl and mix with the semolina and salt. Empty onto a clean work surface and make a deep well in the centre of the flour. Break the eggs into the well. Beat the eggs with a fork, incorporating small amounts of flour as you do so. Mix as much as you can with the fork, and then combine it fully with your hands. Knead for 10 minutes, until you have a smooth and elastic dough. Form into a ball shape, wrap with cling film and rest for 30–40 minutes in a cool place. Cut into pieces, roll out and shape as needed.

375g type '00' flour
125g semolina
½ teaspoon salt
5 eggs

EGGLESS PASTA

**MAKES ENOUGH FOR
4 PEOPLE**

Combine the flour and salt in a large bowl. Make a well in the centre and stream in the warm water, mixing with a fork. When it starts to come together, combine it fully with your hands. Knead for a few minutes, then transfer to a clean, lightly floured work surface and knead for 10 minutes, until you have a smooth and elastic dough. Cover with a clean cloth and let the dough rest for 10 minutes before cutting into pieces, rolling out and shaping as needed.

400g type '00' flour or
  re-milled semolina
½ teaspoon salt
200ml warm water

PASTA ALLA SPOLETINA
SPOLETO PASTA

This pasta dish is based on one from Osteria del Matto in Spoleto. The restaurant is owned by Filippo Proietti, whose mother Santina has had this recipe in her family for generations, and for which she uses strangozzi. The way that Santina and Filippo have shared this recipe tells us lots about Italian home cooking: Santina is more than reluctant to give quantities, believing that we should use whatever is to hand, be it more or less garlic or tomatoes. Filippo takes it one step further: ' If you have lots of tomatoes and you're in a tomato mood, then add them all; if the tomatoes aren't good that day, then don't. I can't be the judge of your tomatoes or your frame of mind.' They both also insist that cheese has no place in this, which makes it traditionally vegan.

Use the quantities given here as a starting point, and don't feel obliged to search out Umbrian strangozzi. Travel to another region if you wish, or perhaps try strozzapretti (which means 'priest stranglers' but we won't judge) or even casarecce. In fact, do as Santina does and make this dish your own.

SERVES 4

6 ripe tomatoes
400g pasta
extra-virgin olive oil
2 garlic cloves, chopped
a large handful of flat-leaf
    parsley, chopped
1 red chilli, sliced (optional)
salt

Submerge the tomatoes in boiling water and leave for 1 minute to loosen the skins. Remove with a slotted spoon and when cool enough to handle, remove and discard the skins and squeeze each tomato to extract most of the seeds (you don't need to fully deseed). Roughly chop the flesh and set aside.

Bring a pan of salted water to the boil and add the pasta. Cook according to the packet instructions, until al dente.

Meanwhile, heat some olive oil in a pan over a medium–low heat. Add the garlic and parsley and fry gently until softened but not browned. Increase the heat and add the skinned tomatoes and the chilli, if using. Cook for 4–5 minutes, until everything is softened and amalgamated.

Drain the cooked pasta and add it to the pan with the tomato mixture. Mix to combine and serve immediately.

PASTA AL LIMONE
LEMON PASTA

I have very fond memories of Ischia, an island off Naples. I was only three when my parents took me there, and it was my first taste of Italy. I remember a bakery selling doughnuts wrapped in beautifully bright tissue paper, being allowed to help throw dough in the pizzeria and playing with the Italian boys on the beach. There were also beautifully fragrant lemons: my father's G&T and trips to the *gelateria* come first to my mind.

My last visit was decades ago but my friend Jane Baxter visited recently, returning with a notebook of culinary discoveries. This is based on her interpretation of a local pasta dish. The key is to use very good lemons, ones that will transport you to the sunshine of the Ischian coast.

SERVES 4

Heat the olive oil in a large frying pan over a low heat. Add the shallots and sweat gently with the honey and lemon zest for 5 minutes, stirring from time to time, until the shallots have softened.

Add the double cream and whisk to combine, then bring to a simmer and cook very gently for a further 2 minutes, until heated thoroughly.

Meanwhile, cook the tagliarini or other long, thin pasta in plenty of salted water according to the packet instructions, until just tender. Drain, reserving about 100ml of the cooking water. Sprinkle the lemon juice over the pasta.

Add the pecorino to the lemon-flavoured cream and stir well. Tip in the pasta and cook gently together for 1 minute, adding a little of the reserved cooking liquid to let down the sauce, if needed. Season well with salt and pepper, stir through the shredded basil leaves and serve immediately.

4 tablespoons extra-virgin olive oil
3 shallots, finely chopped
1 teaspoon runny honey
finely grated zest of 2 unwaxed lemons and 2 tablespoons lemon juice
200ml double cream
400g dried tagliarini, tagliatelle or other long, thin pasta
75g vegetarian pecorino
a small bunch of basil leaves, shredded
salt and freshly ground black pepper

BUSIATE ALLA TRAPANESE

PASTA WITH TRAPANESE PESTO

The classic pasta shape for serving with Pesto Trapanese (see page 163) is busiate. These are long and twirly pieces of pasta, traditionally made by wrapping the dough around knitting needles. You can find busiate online or in Italian delicatessens. Otherwise Enzo Olivieri, chef–owner of Tasting Sicily in London, suggests using fusilli 'because you want the sauce to be trapped in the pasta shapes'. Pesto Trapanese is a satisfyingly creamy sauce – albeit with no cream. Those Sicilian almonds can take the credit for that.

SERVES 4

1 quantity of Trapanese pesto
   (see page 163)
400g busiate or fusilli
50g flaked almonds,
   lightly toasted
vegetarian Italian hard cheese,
   grated (optional)

Cook the pasta according to the packet directions until just al dente. Meanwhile, put the pesto in a pan and heat it up gently. Drain the pasta and add it to the pan with the pesto, stirring until coated.

Spoon the pasta equally onto 4 serving plates, then sprinkle over the toasted almonds. Scatter over some cheese, if you wish.

TROFIE CON PATATE, FAGIOLINI E PESTO
PASTA WITH POTATOES, GREEN BEANS AND PESTO

This dish is a Ligurian classic and is an ideal vehicle for the region's basil pesto. The combination of two starchy carbohydrates may seem counter-intuitive, but it works. The shape of the trofie pasta traps the pesto, the boiled potatoes absorb the flavour of the basil oil and the green beans add freshness.

Note that some Italians put the potatoes on to boil, then add the beans and then the pasta to the same pot. You can do this if you're confident about judging the cooking times of your vegetables, but be careful not to let the potatoes go mushy, especially as they'll also heat up in the pan with the pesto.

SERVES 4

Bring a pan of salted water to the boil and add the potatoes. Boil for about 10–20 minutes, or until just tender, then drain. When they're cool enough to handle, peel them and cut them into thin slices. Set aside.

Bring a separate pan of salted water to the boil and add the beans. Cook for about 8–10 minutes, or until tender, then drain and immediately refresh in very cold water. Drain again and set aside.

Cook the pasta according to the packet instructions, until al dente. Reserve a cup of the cooking water before draining.

Return the pasta to the pan, add the sliced potatoes and beans and the pesto. Mix well to combine and heat through, adding some of the reserved cooking water if the sauce requires loosening. (Do note that the higher the cheese content of your pesto, the more likely it is to stick to the bottom of the pan.) Spoon into serving bowls and add a final spoonful of pesto on the top of each serving, if you wish.

4 medium waxy potatoes
200g green beans,
    stalks removed
350g trofie or other pasta, such
    as trenette or linguine
4 generous tablespoons basil
    pesto (see page 162), plus
    extra to serve (optional)

PENNE IN SALSA DI NOCI
PENNE IN WALNUT SAUCE

Walnuts are found throughout Italy, as are beautiful bowls and other wooden objects made from their tree's wood. The nuts are found in various dishes and the first pasta I came across with a walnut sauce was a ricotta-filled ravioli, but linguine, spaghetti and penne (as here) are all good choices, too.

A walnut sauce is often made with cream, but I like it as more of a pesto, albeit with walnuts and parsley instead of pine nuts and basil. Some people blanch their walnuts to remove the papery skin, but it is not essential.

SERVES 4

300g shelled walnuts, roughly chopped
30g vegetarian Italian hard cheese, finely grated
20g parsley
½ garlic clove
1 teaspoon salt, plus extra to season
a pinch of black pepper, plus extra to season
about 8 tablespoons extra-virgin olive oil, plus extra to serve
350g penne pasta

Reserve a small quantity of the chopped walnuts for garnish. Put the remainder, along with the cheese, parsley, garlic and salt and pepper in a blender. Blitz to combine. Add enough oil to make quite a loose sauce. Transfer the sauce to a pan large enough to hold the cooked pasta and set aside.

Bring a pan of salted water to the boil and add the penne. Cook according to the packet instructions until just al dente. Reserve a few spoonfuls of the cooking water, then drain.

While the pasta is cooking, gently heat through the walnut sauce on a low heat.

Loosen the walnut sauce with a little of the reserved pasta cooking water and adjust the seasoning, if necessary. Add the pasta to the pan with the sauce and stir to coat. Serve immediately sprinkled with an extra drizzle of olive oil and a few sprinkled chopped walnuts.

CACIO E PEPE

Some Italian dishes are so well known that we don't need a translation, and in recent years, *cacio e pepe* pasta has entered that category. Making it at home requires organisation and speed, but once everything is set up and you're ready to go, it really is Roman fast food.

This recipe comes from Andrea di Bello who was born and raised in Rome and who says, 'It's a must in every Roman family.' His grandmother (who, he says, makes the best *cacio e pepe* he's ever tasted) has passed on her hints and tips for success: the pasta has to be cooked in far less water (500ml of water for every 100g of pasta) than you might usually use, because the sauce relies on a heavy concentration of starch in the cooking water. If you find this sauce too rich, add some lemon juice.

SERVES 4

Have a medium-sized mixing bowl warmed and ready to one side.

Bring 2.25 litres of water to the boil in a large pan. Add the salt and, when it has dissolved, add the pasta. Place a lid on the pan until the water returns to the boil. Then, remove the lid and cook the pasta according to the packet instructions, until al dente (usually about 10–12 minutes).

Meanwhile, put another large saucepan on low–medium heat. Crack the peppercorns in a mortar, add to the pan and then toast for about 4 minutes. Add 2–3 small ladlefuls of the boiling pasta water and stir to combine. Leave on the heat.

When the pasta is almost cooked (about 2 minutes before the time given in the packet instructions), use tongs or a slotted spoon to transfer it to the pan with the pepper. Do not discard the water because you need its starchiness to make the sauce. Add a couple of further small ladlefuls of the pasta cooking water and stir with a wooden spoon. Set aside for the water to evaporate. (Reserve the remaining pasta cooking water.)

Add 1 or 2 small ladlefuls of the pasta cooking water to your prepared, warmed bowl. Stir in the grated cheese, then blitz with a handheld stick blender to a smooth sauce. Add further cooking water if required – you're aiming for a creamy consistency, free of lumps and not too runny.

Once the water has evaporated from the pasta, reduce the heat and stir in the pecorino sauce, adding a little extra cooking water if it has become too thick and lemon juice if you feel it's too rich. Once the pasta is coated in the creamy sauce, serve immediately with extra grated pecorino and black pepper should you wish.

20g salt
450g dried tonarelli or spaghetti
1 generous tablespoon of black peppercorns, plus optional extra, cracked, to serve
400g vegetarian pecorino, finely grated, plus optional extra to serve
juice of 1 lemon (optional)

LASAGNE VEGETARIANE
VEGETARIAN LASAGNE

The conventional oven-baked meat and *besciamella* (béchamel) sauce version of lasagne, *lasagne al forno* is eaten around the world. These individual vegetable ones take a little bit of time and effort to assemble but they are lighter and perfect for summertime. If you want, use a mix of different coloured lasagne sheets.

SERVES 4

2 very large aubergines
extra-virgin olive oil
2 pinches of dried oregano
500g cherry tomatoes, halved
1 small aubergine, cut into 20 fine
    slices with a knife or mandolin
200g ricotta
a small handful of basil, leaves
    picked and finely chopped
a small handful of flat-leaf
    parsley, finely chopped
500g spinach
8 dried or fresh lasagne sheets
    (about 18cm x 8cm each)
salt and freshly ground
    black pepper

Heat the oven to 200°C/180°C fan/gas mark 6.

Cut the two large aubergines in half lengthways. Score the flesh, and place them cut-sides upwards in a baking dish. Drizzle with a little oil and sprinkle over the oregano. Season with salt and pepper, then cover with foil and bake for about 45 minutes, until the aubergine flesh is soft. (You may need more or less time, depending on the precise size and shape of your aubergine.)

Meanwhile, place the tomato halves cut-sides upwards on a baking tray. Drizzle with olive oil and season with salt and pepper. Bake for about 20 minutes, keeping an eye on them so that the edges don't burn. When they are cooked and very soft but still intact, remove them and set aside.

While the tomatoes are baking, heat 1 tablespoon of olive oil in a frying pan over a medium heat. Add the aubergine slices in batches and fry on both sides until golden and crunchy but not burnt. Set aside on kitchen paper.

When the baked aubergines are ready, remove them from the oven, spoon the flesh into a bowl and discard the skins. Reduce the oven heat to 140°C/120°C fan/gas mark 1. Cut up the cooked aubergine, mash it with a fork and leave to cool. When cool, mix in the ricotta, then the basil, parsley and a drizzle of olive oil – or enough to make the mixture spreadable.

Put the spinach in a pan, season with salt and pepper and place over a medium–low heat. Allow the leaves to wilt, then remove them from the heat, leave to cool slightly and squeeze out as much water as possible.

Place each vegetable into its own dish and cover with foil. Return to the oven to keep warm while you cook the pasta.

Bring a pan of salted water to the boil. Add the lasagne sheets and cook according to the packet instructions until they are al dente. Remove

from the water with a slotted fish slice and set aside on kitchen paper to drain. When cool enough to handle, cut them in half so that you have squares not rectangles of pasta.

Assemble each lasagne portion individually on a plate: begin with a sheet of pasta, then spread on the aubergine and ricotta mash, add some spinach, then add a few tomatoes. Alternate these, finishing with a pasta sheet with a small amount of aubergine mash on top. If you wish, place each plate in the oven to keep warm while you assemble the next. When they are all assembled, garnish with the fried aubergine discs and place any leftover tomatoes around the edge. Serve immediately.

RAVIOLONE AL TUORLO DI UOVO CON ASPARAGI

EGG-YOLK RAVIOLI WITH ASPARAGUS

I first ate egg-yolk ravioli at a restaurant in Barolo, Piedmont. It wasn't a terribly fancy place, but cutting into a raviolo only for delicious egg yolk to run out was quite a moment. In truth, making these is far easier than the drama of eating them suggests – you just need to be gentle.

Many years ago, the great chef Franco Taruschio told Jane Baxter and me that he made these ravioli using Chinese wonton wrappers. Here is Jane's interpretation of that suggestion and it works a dream. Of course, you can use fresh pasta sheets, or even use bought fresh lasagne sheets, if you prefer. I've given both options below.

SERVES 4

1–2 tablespoons extra-virgin olive oil
500g asparagus, trimmed
1 teaspoon thyme leaves
8 wonton wrappers or 4 fresh lasagne sheets
1 teaspoon cornflour, mixed with a little water to make a paste (if using wonton wrappers)
4 individual egg yolks
2–3 tablespoons rapeseed oil, for shallow frying (if using wonton wrappers)
20g vegetarian Italian hard cheese, grated
1 tablespoon chopped chives
salt and freshly ground black pepper

Heat the oil over a medium heat in a frying pan that will hold all the asparagus in a layer (or cook in batches). Add the asparagus, thyme and seasoning. Cook for about 5 minutes (depending on the size of your spears), turning, to ensure that the spears are heated evenly, then cover with a lid for 1 minute, or until they are just tender.

While the asparagus is cooking make the ravioli.

If you're using wonton wrappers: Lay 4 wonton wrappers on a clean tea towel. Brush the cornflour paste around the edges. Carefully place an egg yolk into the centre of each wonton, then gently place another wonton wrapper on top of each yolk. Press firmly around the edges to seal completely. Heat the oil in a shallow frying pan over a medium–high heat. Add a single raviolo to the pan and fry for 1 minute, turning half way through cooking, to make sure both sides are crisp. Remove from the oil and set aside to drain on kitchen paper, then fry the others.

If you're using lasagne sheets: Cut each lasagne sheet in half to give 8 approximately 9cm squares. Place 4 of the squares on a clean tea towel. Carefully place an egg yolk into the centre of each pasta square. Brush water around the edges, then gently place another pasta square on top of each yolk. Press firmly around the edges to seal completely. Bring a pan of salted water to the boil. Gently transfer the ravioli into the water and cook for about 4 minutes, until the pasta is al dente. Remove carefully with a slotted spoon and set aside to drain on kitchen paper.

Divide the cooked asparagus between 4 plates. Top each plate with 1 raviolo and sprinkle with the grated cheese and the chopped chives. Serve immediately.

CICERI E TRIA
PASTA AND CHICKPEAS

Pasta with beans is a well-known Italian pairing. What makes this recipe, from the Salento in southern Puglia, special is that some of the pasta is fried. I first ate this in the stunning baroque city of Lecce at a rustic trattoria called Cucina Casereccia. Anna Carmela Perrone, its chef-owner whose own recipe inspired this one, told me that among all the Salentine dishes, this one is her favourite.

SERVES 6

Drain the chickpeas and bring a pan of salted water to the boil. Add the chickpeas, garlic, celery and bay (which Anna believes aid digestion of the chickpeas), then reduce the heat and simmer for about 1 hour, periodically skimming away the scum that rises to the surface, until tender. Then, drain and discard the garlic, celery and bay.

While the chickpeas are cooking, make the pasta using the flour, water and ½ teaspoon of salt (see page 127). Cut the pasta into 3 pieces. Using a pasta machine, roll out a piece at a time, starting with the widest setting, passing the pasta through a couple of times before moving to the next setting down. Finish at the second to last setting. Cut into small, short strips similar in size to a stick of chewing gum. Lightly sprinkle over some semolina, move them through your hands so that they separate, and leave to dry out for 30 minutes.

Shake any excess flour from the pasta. Heat the oil in a large frying pan over a medium–high heat. Take a quarter of the pasta and fry it for 3–4 minutes in batches, turning it so that it cooks all over and becomes lightly golden. Set each batch aside to drain on kitchen paper while you fry the next.

Bring a pan of salted water to the boil, add the rest of the pasta and cook briefly, so that it is softened, but undercooked.

Drain most of the oil from the pan, leaving a couple of tablespoons. Place over a gentle heat, then add the fried pasta, boiled pasta and the chickpeas and sauté very quickly, until everything is warmed through and the boiled pasta has cooked to your liking. Serve immediately seasoned with freshly ground black pepper.

500g dried chickpeas,
    soaked overnight
2 garlic cloves
1 celery stick, halved
2 bay leaves
500g type '00' white flour
250ml warm water
a handful of semolina
200ml extra-virgin olive oil
salt and freshly ground
    black pepper

I PIZZOCCHERI DI MAMMA LUCINDA
MAMMA LUCINDA'S PIZZOCCHERI

A short distance south of the Alps in northern Lombardy is the Valtellina, a valley that heads eastwards from Lake Como. It's a place that is dear to my heart, with beautiful scenery, charming hillside villages and hard-working but fun mountain people who produce some excellent cheese and wines. North of Tirano are ski resorts such as Bormio, and this classic buckwheat pasta dish is perfectly rib-sticking after a bracing day on the slopes.

This recipe is based on one by Anna Bertola, who runs the Altavilla trattoria in Bianzone. It is a variation on her mother's way of preparing this traditional dish. Anna is known for her warm welcome and her generous portion sizes.

You can find boxes of dried pizzoccheri pasta in Italian delicatessens and online, but here are the instructions should you wish to make your own.

SERVES 4

FOR THE PIZZOCCHERI
400g buckwheat flour
200g type '00' white flour
½ teaspoon salt
250–350ml water, as needed

or 600g dried pizzoccheri

FOR THE VEGETABLES
200g potatoes, peeled and cut
    into about 2cm cubes
100g Savoy cabbage, cut into
    3cm strips
200g vegetarian cheese that
    melts easily (similar to Valtellina
    Casera or fontina), sliced thinly
100g vegetarian Italian hard
    cheese, grated
100g butter
½ onion, sliced
salt and freshly ground
    black pepper

If you're making the pizzoccheri, combine the two flours and the salt in a bowl. Make a well in the centre and gradually add the water to form a crumbly dough. Knead for about 10 minutes, until the dough is smooth and elastic. Cover and leave to rest for 30 minutes.

Either cut the dough in half and roll each to a thickness of about 3mm with a rolling pin, or divide into smaller balls to pass through a pasta machine. Cut your rolled out pasta into 8cm-wide lengths. Finally, cut these widthways to produce tagliatelle of about 7mm wide. Set aside.

Bring a pan of salted water to the boil. Add the potatoes and cook for about 5 minutes, then add the cabbage. Bring the water back to the boil and cook for 1–2 minutes. Drain and leave in the warm, covered pan.

Heat the oven to 200°C/180°C fan/gas mark 6. In a separate pan of boiling salted water, cook the pasta: about 1–2 minutes for fresh pasta or according to the packet instructions for dried. When the pasta is nearly cooked, turn off the heat. Using a slotted spoon, place a couple of spoonfuls of the pasta in an ovenproof serving dish measuring about 25cm x 32cm. Add a couple of spoonfuls of the vegetables. Lay some of the sliced cheese on top and sprinkle over some of the grated cheese. Continue alternating layers of the pizzoccheri and vegetables and cheese (you should have 2 or 3 layers of each), finishing with a layer of cheese.

Melt the butter in a frying pan over a medium heat. Add the onion and fry for 5 minutes, until browned, then scatter over the top of the pizzoccheri. Cover with foil and place in the oven for about 5–10 minutes, until the cheese has melted. Serve seasoned with freshly ground pepper to taste.

SPAGHETTI ALL'ASSASSINA
ASSASSIN'S SPAGHETTI

Burnt pasta? Who'd have thought that this would be sanctioned, or even applauded in Italy? Yet in Bari, Puglia's capital, there's considerable enthusiasm for this dish. If the classic pasta dish of spaghetti *aglio, olio, peperoncino* is one you find irresistible, then you'll probably enjoy this one too. The textural surprise from the burnt bits of spaghetti form a feature, served as they are in pride of place on the top of the pile of pasta. Cooking in an iron pan is traditional, but the pasta will catch even in a non-stick pan, as long as enough of the sauce has been absorbed – the texture should be rather dry.

SERVES 4

In a large non-stick frying pan heat the oil on a low–medium heat. Add the garlic and fry gently for 3–4 minutes, until golden. Remove the garlic from the pan and discard.

Add the chopped chilli to the oil and fry gently for 1 minute, until softened. Turn down the heat and add the cherry tomatoes (be careful because the oil may spit), then increase the heat to medium and stir the tomatoes until they start to break up (about 3–4 minutes). Add the passata and mix to combine, then season with salt and pepper. Keep warm on a gentle heat.

Separately bring a large pan of heavily salted water to the boil. Hold all of the spaghetti in your hand at the top of the bundle. Carefully immerse the bottom of the spaghetti in the boiling water and press around the bottom of the pan so that as it softens it all becomes submerged and the lengths remain unbroken. Stir to stop the spaghetti sticking together and cook for half the recommended time on the packet. Using tongs, remove the pasta from the water and transfer it to the pan with the tomatoes. Discard the cooking water.

Increase the heat so that the sauce simmers and stir intermittently until the pasta is cooked to your liking and has absorbed the sauce. Increase the heat to its highest setting. After a while (the exact time will depend on how dry your pasta is and the type of pan you're using), the pasta will catch on the bottom of the pan. You're aiming for a mixture of cooked pasta with some caught, somewhat burnt pasta.

Turn out the pasta onto a dish so that the burnt spaghetti is on the top and divide into 4 equal portions. Serve with chilli oil for people to add if they'd like their dish a little punchier.

5 tablespoons extra-virgin olive oil
1 garlic clove, peeled
1 red chilli, finely chopped
200g cherry tomatoes, halved
400ml passata (see page 159)
400g spaghetti
homemade chilli oil, to serve (optional; see page 167)
salt and freshly ground black pepper

CONDIMENTS

PINZIMONIO

The Italian version of crudités and a dip is an exercise in simplicity, and an enjoyable way to appreciate spring and summer vegetables when their flavours are at their brightest. Traditionally, a bowl of seasoned oil (the *pinzimonio*) is served to each diner, but if you have a couple of distinct oils that you like, then prepare one of each. Think of contrasting characteristics, so perhaps a grassy oil alongside a peppery one.

You don't need to prepare a large assortment of vegetables – I know Italians who choose just celery and spring onions. The selection below is one I often assemble, sometimes with cucumbers and small lettuce leaves too.

SERVES 1

2 small carrots, halved or cut
    into batons
2 spring onions, trimmed
    and halved
½ small fennel bulb, quartered
2 celery sticks, trimmed, halved,
    and cut lengthways if wide
2 radishes, trimmed and halved
¼ red or yellow pepper,
    deseeded and cut into strips
2 tablespoons extra-virgin
    olive oil
salt and freshly ground
    black pepper

Arrange the vegetables on an individual serving plate. If it's a very hot day, rest the plate on a bowl with some ice to keep the vegetables cool.

Place some salt and pepper into a small bowl and pour the oil into it. Serve with instructions to scoop some of the salt and pepper from the bottom of the bowl when dipping.

GIARDINIERA
MIXED PICKLED VEGETABLES

Jars of *giardiniera* pickles are beautiful. Shelves of them, with their multi-coloured contents, are an arresting sight. The recipe is flexible (this one originates from Emilia-Romagna), and you can easily change the proportions depending upon your favourite or most abundant veg. Some people jazz up their pickles with chilli, but I like the taste of the individual vegetables to shine through. Great with cheeses, in sandwiches and in rice salad (see page 71), they do a lot more than just look good.

**2 X 1 LITRE STERILISED JARS
OR 4 X 500ML JARS**

150g squash, peeled, deseeded
and cut into small cubes
150g carrots, peeled and cut into
thick rounds
150g celery, trimmed, destringed
and cut into strips
150g spring onions, outer leaves
removed, trimmed and cut
crossways into 4 pieces
150g green beans, trimmed and
cut into halves or thirds
300g cauliflower florets
150g red peppers, deseeded
and cut into strips
150g yellow or green peppers,
deseeded and cut into strips

FOR THE PICKLING LIQUID
750ml white wine vinegar
200ml dry white wine
1 bay leaf
15g coarse salt
15g caster sugar
½ teaspoon black peppercorns
4 tablespoon extra-virgin olive oil

Make the pickling liquid. Pour 750ml of water into a large pan and add the vinegar, wine, bay leaf, salt, sugar and peppercorns. Place over a medium heat. Bring to a lively simmer for 3–4 minutes, stirring, until the salt and sugar have dissolved.

Add the vegetables to the pan so that they soften and the flavours of the pickling liquid infuse. Leave them to reach the level of crunch that you like. I cook for approximately the following times: the squash about 11 minutes; carrots and celery 7 minutes; spring onions 6 minutes; green beans 5 minutes; cauliflower 4 minutes; and peppers 3 minutes.

Remove the vegetables from the pickling liquid using a slotted spoon and put them in the prepared jars. Bring the pickling liquid to the boil for a couple of minutes.

Meanwhile, bring a large pan of water to the boil.

Divide the oil equally between the jars of vegetables, then top up with pickling liquid to a finger-width from the rim. Seal the jars and sterilise them again by boiling in a pan of water for 20 minutes.

Leave for 1 week before eating. Store the jars in a cool, dry place for up to 3 months; once opened, keep in the fridge for up to a fortnight.

PASSATA
TOMATO PASSATA

The traditional, and Italians will say the best tomato for making passata is the San Marzano, a variety from Naples. *Passare* means to pass through, and this sauce is passed through a sieve to remove the seeds. It is made when tomatoes are at their sun-ripened best, then stored for use throughout the year for pasta sauces, pizza toppings, bruschette and so on – until the next tomato harvest arrives.

This quantity will make a couple of medium-sized jars, depending on how ripe and juicy the tomatoes are. You can buy passata machines into which you load the tomatoes, turn a handle and the pips are separated from the pulp. It is a lot easier, and more fun than manually forcing kilos of tomatoes through a sieve. I find my machine invaluable.

Note that both the salt and the oil act as preservatives, as well as flavouring. You can add other flavours too, such as basil, but keeping things neutral makes the passata more adaptable.

MAKES ABOUT 2 X 400ML STERILISED JARS

Sterilise your jars by boiling them in water for 10 minutes and leaving to air dry.

Place the whole tomatoes in a bowl and pour over boiling water. Leave for a few minutes as this makes removing the skins easier. Carefully remove the tomatoes one by one, and peel, discarding the skins.

Put the tomatoes into a passata machine, or chop roughly and push them through a sieve set over a bowl. Repeat a few times in order to extract the maximum amount of pulp you can. Add salt to taste.

Divide the pulp equally between your sterilised jars, top with olive oil to create a seal and secure the lid. Place the jars in a tall pan, wrapping a tea towel between them so that they don't crash against each other and crack. Pour boiling water over and around the jars and simmer for 10 minutes (this is a water-bath method of preserving). Leave the water to cool before removing the jars. Label with the month of production and store in a cool place for up to a year. Always check that there is no mould before using.

3kg ripe tomatoes, preferably San Marzano
2–3 teaspoons fine salt
6 tablespoons extra-virgin olive oil

SEVEN TIPS FOR USING PASSATA

- Add chopped onions and garlic to make the simplest pasta sauce.

- Use as a base on which to lay stuffed, rolled vegetables (such as the Involtini on page 121) or aubergines, thinly sliced, cooked on a griddle pan, and then wrapped around a spoonful of ricotta mixed with chopped herbs.

- Heat through with some crushed garlic to make a sauce for green beans.

- Add herbs such as basil, which is a classic, or some rosemary. If you'd prefer heat, mix in chilli pepper.

- Use as a sauce for potato gnocchi, with some grated cheese to finish.

- Keep to hand for a baked *lasagne al forno*, perhaps with squash and some goat's cheese.

- Add to casseroles, stews and braises and in caponata-style dishes (substitute the vegetables on page 159 with fennel, courgettes or carrots).

SEVEN TIPS FOR USING PESTO

- Although the classic Genovese Pesto is made with basil, using other herbs and leaves has become increasingly popular. Tarragon, wild garlic or rocket all work well. Or even roasted, peeled and deseeded red peppers.

- Add more oil to loosen your pesto for use as a dressing, perhaps for a variation on potato salad.

- Spread on toasted bread before topping with vegetarian mozzarella and sliced tomatoes, or cooked mushrooms.

- If pine nuts aren't available, use almonds (as in Pesto Trapanese, see page 163) or skinned walnuts.

- Drizzle over roasted vegetables, such as courgettes or peppers.

- Mix with ricotta to make a dip.

- Blind bake puff-pastry squares, top with a thin layer of pesto and roasted tomato halves for the simplest of summer vegetable tarts.

PESTO GENOVESE
BASIL PESTO

Pesto is internationally popular, especially the classic from Genova, made with basil. Homemade pesto is so much more vibrant than commercial versions, which often use sunflower oil (instead of olive) and sad cheese. Making your own allows you to customise it: leave out the cheese (as sometimes happens in Liguria) if you're vegan; add more or less garlic or oil depending on your preference or how you're going to use it. A spoonful added to a minestrone is a classic for a reason, and the Ligurian dish of pasta with beans, potatoes and pesto is on page 137.

Most Italians I know insist on pounding the ingredients with a pestle in a mortar (a basil-perfumed kitchen is a bonus), although many professional Italian chefs recommend using a blender. There is also debate over whether to cut or tear the basil leaves. It is often said that cutting them makes them turn brown, but Gillian Riley states that Harold McGee denies this. I certainly won't dispute what either of these greats says, but I've always torn the leaves – old habits die hard.

**MAKES 1 X 200ML
STERILISED JAR**

1 large garlic clove,
    roughly chopped
100g basil leaves, roughly torn
25g pine nuts, toasted
10g coarse sea salt flakes
100ml extra-virgin olive oil
20g vegetarian Italian hard
    cheese, finely grated

Put your mortar on a folded tea towel to keep it from moving. Little by little, add the garlic, basil, pine nuts and salt to the mortar, pounding and crushing with the pestle between each addition. Gradually add the oil and cheese, a healthy splash and a pinch at a time until you have a thick paste. Transfer the mixture to a jar, top with any remaining oil and seal with the lid.

Store in the fridge and use within 4–5 days.

PESTO TRAPANESE

TRAPANESE PESTO

This pesto, sometimes called *pesto alla Siciliana*, comes from the coastal town of Trapani, to the west of Palermo in northern Sicily. There is a cable car with fabulous views that travels up to the magical hill town of Erice. Blessed with soothing breezes in the summer heat, it is also home to the *pasticceria* of Maria Grammatico, its gastronomic star known far and wide for her almond pastes and marzipans. The almonds in this part of Sicily are like none I've ever tasted: exquisitely creamy and packed full of flavour, they're found in numerous dishes, including this pesto.

This recipe is based on one that Sicilian chef Enzo Olivieri uses in his London kitchen. He says that it should be made with a pestle and mortar, but he gives his blessing if we'd rather use a blender. Although this pesto is most usually used as a pasta sauce, Enzo also combines it with breadcrumbs and uses it as a filling for aubergine or courgette involtini. He imports his almonds from Sicily – the rest of us just have to find the best we can.

SERVES 4

Place all the ingredients except the oil in a blender (or mortar) and blitz (or pound) to a rough texture – you want to retain small pieces of almond. Stir in the oil to combine.

Use as soon as you can.

1 garlic clove
3–4 mint leaves
50g flaked almonds
100g vine cherry
　　tomatoes, halved
a large handful of basil,
　　leaves picked
a pinch of chilli flakes
a large pinch of salt
100ml extra-virgin olive oil

Clockwise from left: Olio Santo (see page 167); Giardiniera (see page 158); Passata (see page 159); Pesto Trapanese (see page 163); Pesto Genovese (see page 162); Salmoriglio (see page 166); Gremolata (see page 166)

GREMOLATA

Gremolata is the simplest trio of flavours and yet adds a spring to the step of any dish it touches. Well known as the final garnish to the veal dish *ossobuco*, it also works a charm on vegetable dishes. Try a swirl on creamy soups (such as parsnip or squash); or on roasted carrots, sautéed greens, or vegetable and polenta dishes. It is also good added to vegetable and cheese pastas. I've also seen it sprinkled on avocado toast, if that's your thing. Because all the ingredients are raw, they need to be brightly fresh.

MAKES ENOUGH TO GARNISH A MAIN COURSE FOR 4 PEOPLE

2 garlic cloves, halved
finely grated zest of 1 large
  unwaxed lemon
a large handful of flat-leaf
  parsley leaves, finely chopped

Remove and discard the central core of the halved garlic cloves, then chop the garlic as finely as you can. Add the lemon zest, and chop both again so that the zest is small. Transfer to a small bowl, add the parsley and stir to combine. Sprinkle on top of vegetable dishes that need some zing.

SALMORIGLIO

Most usually drizzled over fish dishes, salmoriglio is also a good dressing for roasted vegetables, such as tomatoes, aubergines, peppers, courgettes, squash and fennel, or even as a dip for celery sticks. The condiment hails from Sicily and is traditionally made using seawater ('but we'll use salt', says Enzo Olivieri, a London-based chef from Palermo). This recipe makes enough to liberally dress a large plate of roasted vegetables with some left over, depending on how generous you like your dressing. Although it tastes more vibrant when used immediately, it will keep in a cool place for a day or so.

MAKES ENOUGH TO DRESS A MAIN COURSE

2 garlic cloves
juice of 1 lemon
1 tablespoon dried oregano
a large pinch of salt
a large pinch of black pepper
150–200ml extra-virgin olive oil

Peel and squash the garlic, using the flat side of a large knife – this will release its flavour, but you'll still be able to remove it intact.

Place the garlic in a bowl with the lemon juice, oregano, salt and pepper. Whisk in 150ml of the olive oil, then taste. If it's too acidic, add more oil (the acidity will depend on the size and juiciness of your lemon). Remove and discard the garlic. Use as a condiment for cooked or raw vegetables.

OLIO SANTO PICCANTE FATTO IN CASA
HOT HOMEMADE CHILLI OIL

Olio santo literally means 'holy oil' and is indeed venerated in Calabria. Those from other regions in Italy's southern Mezzogiorno may not think that adding fiery chilli oil to dishes is necessarily an improvement, but most Calabrese think otherwise. Filippo Cogliandro, a chef in the city of Reggio Calabria, explains that 'Olio santo is nothing other than spicy-hot oil, so-called because it is considered sacred.' He uses it for seasoning bruschette, soups, pulses, sauces and vegetables and as a condiment for pasta. Although Vittorio Cavaliere, a friend from Puglia, isn't as effusive: 'Olio santo is so-called because in Calabria, where it was born, it is added to every plate of food as if it is a sacred ritual, and it is thought that it improves food. Not for me it doesn't.' Regardless of whether you like to liberally pour it over everything, or use it more discerningly, it's useful to have at hand for when you do want to add a bit of a kick to something.

MAKES 1 X 200ML STERILISED JAR

6 red chillies
25g fine salt
150–200ml white wine vinegar
150–200ml extra-virgin olive oil

Wash the chillies and dry them with a clean cloth. Take care not to touch your eyes (wear gloves if you are particularly sensitive). Remove the stalks from the chillies and use scissors to cut them into rings of about 1cm.

Put the chilli pieces in a bowl and pour over the salt. Mix to combine, then cover with a cloth and leave to rest for around 10–12 hours, stirring the mixture from time to time.

Drain off all the liquid from the salted chillies, then squeeze them and pat with kitchen paper so that you remove as much liquid as you can and they are as dry as possible.

Put the chillies in another bowl, cover with white wine vinegar, stir and leave to rest for about 10–15 minutes. Drain off and discard the vinegar, then squeeze and pat the chillies with kitchen paper again.

Spoon the chilli pieces into the jar or wide-rimmed bottle, and press them down to give a good 5mm gap at the top of the jar. Fill the jar with extra-virgin olive oil and leave to settle for 1 hour. Finally, top up with a little more oil and seal firmly with the lid.

Store the olio santo in a cool, dark place for a few days. Once opened, store in the fridge. As you use the oil, top it up a little bit, but not so that you dilute the flavour too much. However, it's important that the chillies don't become exposed to the air, so as you use the oil, as soon as a chilli pops out uncovered, remove it and discard.

INDEX

ACKNOWLEDGEMENTS

Like most food projects, a cookbook is a collaborative effort and I am so grateful to all the brilliant people who have been part of this one. Huge thanks to the exceptional team at Absolute: Jon Croft for contacting me; Meg Boas for the commission; Emily North for unwavering support and unparalleled efficiency; Anika Schulze, and Marie O'Shepherd for the beautiful design (while creating the even more beautiful Piper).

The photoshoot team was the best: the gifted Mike Cooper and his fab studio (if only there'd been room in the book for one of his salad cream ideas); Matt Inwood for design flair and the ability to identify the perfect prop at 100 paces; Genevieve Taylor for keeping the beat going amid pans, sequins and her gorgeous ceramics; Adam O'Shepherd for boundless creative energy despite being a sleep-deprived new father. Your joint appetite for cinnamon buns is unequalled. Bravo!

A heartfelt *grazie* to all the Italian food producers and chefs who have spent time over the past decades generously sharing their expertise with me. Your stories, our adventures and the meals we've enjoyed together have taught me so much about Italy's regional food and cooking: Pietro Zito; Marco Caprai and Salvatore Denaro; Gabriele Lafranconi; Andrea di Bello; Enzo Olivieri; Alice Delcourt and Danilo Ingannamorte; Fernando Aldighieri; Marco Sposino; Carmine Cataldo; Filippo Cogliandro; Anna Carmela Perrone; Patrizia Moretti and family; the team at Eat Jesolo; Anna Bertola; Santina, Rungruedee and Filippo Proietti; Cesare Battisti; and Peppe Zullo.

My friends who have helped in countless ways: Anna and Vittorio Cavaliere for your warm welcomes and eagerness to disclose insider knowledge; Emma Lundie for Sardinian savvy; Paolo Arrigo for chat, seeds and berets; the party-loving Terni crew of Renzo and Paola Franceschini, Andrea Barbaccia and Beppe Neri; Elizabeth Canning for her tireless assistance and encouragement; the unfailingly imaginative Giacomo Mojoli; Caroline Shaw, Jane Livesey and Andrea Bothamley for life-affirming get-togethers over some excellent wines; Anne Eyries who I wish lived nearer; Sandra Merton for her runaway exuberance; Abigail Huges-Jones for ever-dependable and smiling advice; the team at the Abergavenny Food Festival who do so much for food producers – Martin Orbach, Kim Waters, Martha Roberts, Sarah Dickins, Ruth Tudor, Jon Child and William Griffiths; Helen Girgenti and her team at the Italian Chamber of Commerce for invaluable help; Monica Olivieri for bringing Italian pizzazz to London; Rhuaridh Buchanan of Buchanans Cheesemonger for helpful chats; Kate and Richard at Holtwhites Bakery for excellent bread and supplies of ricotta; the great team at Belazu; Urvashi Roe and Tony who provided respite and laughter when recipe testing was overwhelming; the many friends I've made through the Guild of Food Writers, especially the accomplished and convivial Jonathan Woods, Angela Clutton and Charlotte Pike; Kate Hawkings for unquenchable verve and Jane Baxter, my favourite chef and the best person to share a negroni-prefaced meal with in Italy.

Everlasting thanks to my father who, impressively, is still the first person to hit the dance floor. And finally, to my husband Dan, who has been enthusiastically at my side since the start of these recipes. Here's to many more long lunches and late dinners together.

Publisher
Jon Croft

Commissioning Editor
Meg Boas

Senior Editor
Emily North

Art Director
Matt Inwood

Design
Marie O'Shepherd &
Peter Moffat

Junior Designer & Cover Design
Anika Schulze

Photography
Mike Cooper

Photography Assistant
Martin Allen

Home Economist & Food Styling
Genevieve Taylor

Food Styling Assistant
Adam O'Shepherd

Copyeditor
Judy Barratt

Proofreader
Margaret Haynes

Indexer
Zoe Ross

BLOOMSBURY ABSOLUTE

Bloomsbury Publishing Plc
50 Bedford Square, London, WC1B 3DP, UK

BLOOMSBURY, BLOOMSBURY ABSOLUTE, the Diana logo and
the Absolute Press logo are trademarks of Bloomsbury Publishing Plc

First published in Great Britain, 2020

Text © Christine Smallwood, 2020
Photography © Mike Cooper, 2020

A catalogue record for this book is available from the British Library.

Library of Congress Cataloguing-in-Publication data has been
applied for.

ISBN: 9781472974716
ePUB: 9781472974709
ePDF: 9781472974693

2 4 6 8 10 9 7 5 3 1

Printed and bound in China by Toppan Leefung Printing

Bloomsbury Publishing Plc makes every effort to ensure that the
papers used in the manufacture of our books are natural, recyclable
products made from wood grown in well-managed forests. Our
manufacturing processes conform to the environmental regulations
of the country of origin.

To find out more about our authors and books visit
www.bloomsbury.com and sign up for our newsletters.